A Stand on Ecumenism:
The Council's Decree

A Stand on Ecumenism:
The Council's Decree

LORENZ CARDINAL JAEGER

Translated by
HILDA GRAEF

 GEOFFREY CHAPMAN
LONDON—DUBLIN 1965

GEOFFREY CHAPMAN LIMITED
18 High Street, Wimbledon, London S.W.19

GEOFFREY CHAPMAN (IRELAND) LIMITED
5-7 Main Street, Blackrock, Co. Dublin, Eire

Originally published 1965 by Bonifacius Druckerei, Paderborn,
under the title
Das Konzilsdekret 'Über den Ökumenismus'

© translation 1965 Geoffrey Chapman Ltd.
First published this edition 1965

The English text of the decree 'On Ecumenism' and
the constitution 'On the Church' is that published by
C. T. S. London, and is used by permission.

Nihil Obstat: R. D. DERMITIUS FOGARTY, D.D., L.C.L., *Censor deputatus*
Imprimatur: H. GIBNEY, *Vicarius Generalis*
Datum Southwarci die 8a Junii 1965

MADE AND PRINTED IN GREAT BRITAIN BY BLACKIE AND SONS LTD., BISHOPBRIGGS, GLASGOW

Contents

Preface

THE DECREE 'On Ecumenism' shows in what way Catholic Christians share in the world-wide ecumenical movement. Today we cannot even begin to estimate how much the realization of its proposals will contribute to unity among Christians for it strengthens the universality of the ecumenical movement and gives it new impulses. It confirms that conversion of the heart, a more faithful devotion to the gospel and the renewal of the Church's life are the leading motives of all efforts made to promote Christian unity, and directs our attention to essentials in order to prevent us from losing ourselves in external activities. The decree regards the ecumenical movement not so much as due to human initiative but as a work begun by the Holy Spirit. It teaches us to acknowledge that the division of Christendom is a sin and to overcome it by forgiveness and reconciliation. At the same time the whole decree has a strongly eschatological aspect: the Church is the pilgrim people of God, hoping for the return of the Lord. It sees in the ecumenical movement a sign from God that promises us Christ's victory over the powers of sin and discord.

As many streams and rivulets are gathered and clarified in a lake, so the labours of many theologians and ecumenical experts have found their fulfilment in the decree 'On Ecumenism'. It is a fruit of three sessions of the Council, developing from the initial ecumenical discussions in the first, through the constructive discussions of the second to its final form in the third session. The success of the decree will depend on our greater obedience to the Word of God and our more faithful following of Christ.

Introduction

DURING the discussions of the second session of Vatican II, Mgr Elchinger, the coadjutor bishop of Strasbourg, called the decree 'On Ecumenism' a grace and favour of God given to our time. He added: 'All that has ever been said and done in the cause of unity, especially the often very difficult efforts of the forerunners of Catholic ecumenism, seem to culminate in this decree. As an expert has written, in the Church facts or events often serve the truth more effectively than purely doctrinal declarations. This schema can be said to be such a fact.'

After the decree had been promulgated Dr Oscar Cullmann expressed a similar opinion on behalf of the Evangelicals. 'The schema on ecumenism' he said, 'which has been accepted by a surprisingly large majority—the very numbers show that a door has been opened—is, to quote the French Dominican Father Yves Congar, not just a text, but an ecumenical deed. In fact, this is more than the opening of a door: new ground has been broken. No Catholic document has ever spoken of non-Catholic Christians in this way. Every single chapter of this schema bears witness of this . . .'[1]

The decree 'On Ecumenism', whose novelty had already been emphasized by Archbishop Martin of Rouen in his *relatio*, is not a revolutionary document; nevertheless, it

[1] *Materialdienst des Konfessionskundlichen Instituts Bensheim*, 15 (1964) 102.

creates a new ecumenical situation which has to be set forth in detail. The first step is to explain the decree itself and this the present book hopes to do.

Our presentation is limited to what is necessary for an understanding of the schema. For this reason we give neither a history of ecumenism in the Catholic Church, though this was important for the preparation of the decree, nor a full treatment of the work of the Secretariat for Christian Unity, though this has decisively influenced the preparation of the ecumenical side of the Council's work.

We are concerned with the solemnly promulgated decree 'On Ecumenism', not with individual events and measures, not with hopes and disappointments. Cardinal Bea wrote in the periodical *Christ und Welt* of 29 January, 1965: 'Considering matters calmly and objectively, the decree 'On Ecumenism' is a very great and significant result of the third session of the Council. This is so despite a few disappointing occurrences during the last days of the session. These must on no account lead to doubts about the serious intention of advancing the ecumenical cause. Moreover, to one who has taken part in the events and knows the situation, it is clear that under the circumstances developments could not have been very different from what they actually were.' With this in view we shall attempt to clarify in Part One of this book the evolution of the decree 'On Ecumenism' from the first version which was discussed during the second session in 1963, through the second version voted on in the third session to the final decree of 21 November, 1964.

Part Two will explain the individual chapters, articles and paragraphs of the final text. While the second version emerged from the 'votes' of the Fathers during the second session, the final form also contains the 'additions' that had been suggested during the voting in the third session and had been worked over by the Secretariat for Unity. Hence we must explain and evaluate what has actually been achieved and give an exact interpretation of the texts agreed upon during the third session. These, according to the *Neue Zürcher Zeitung* of 23 November, 1964, 'deserve the greatest attention from the whole Christian world'. In the words of the Jesuit Alois Grillmeier: 'These texts show that the windows of the Church have been opened wide, perhaps even wider than could be hoped for at the end of the promising though still inconclusive first session. These texts, approved by the Holy Father and the whole Council, will continue to be effective even when the impressions and moods, the discussions and controversies have long been forgotten. They will be the more effective the more unanimously and energetically they are accepted both by the Council Fathers and by all the faithful.'[1]

In explaining the schema we shall try to determine as accurately as possible the meaning or at least the direction in which the decisions of the Council are to be understood. This will often be made possible by indicating why a certain expression or alteration appears in the text. In other cases the meaning of an individual statement may emerge from the context. The only official text is the Latin original.[2]

According to the custom of many Councils, the official text of the decree quotes only the scriptures, the Fathers of the Church and earlier Councils. References to direct quo-

[1] A. Grillmeier, 'Sorgen und Hoffnungen um das Konzil', in *Stimmen der Zeit* 90 (1965) 288.
[2] The English translation given here is by Rev Austin Carvey, C.T.S., London, 1965.

tations from scripture are given in the text of the decree, other references to scripture, to the Fathers and conciliar documents are given in footnotes.

The text is indebted to many other sources and also occasionally takes account of the more recent theological literature. A knowledge of these sources adds considerably to a scientific study of the decree; hence a list of some of those not mentioned in the decree itself is given in our Appendix. Study of these texts will facilitate understanding of the decree, especially as it follows the lines taken by some of these documents and brings some of their suggestions to realization.

Within the scope of this book it is impossible to name all the sources that have contributed to the decree 'On Ecumenism'. Apart from the results of Catholic ecumenical activity before the Council, these would especially include all the proposals made by the future Council Fathers during the preparation of Vatican II; these are printed in the *Acta et Documenta Concilio Vaticano II apparando* which are still secret. To these would have to be added all the 'votes' on the schema of the Fathers in Council, whether delivered orally or in writing, which can here be considered only as their results are reflected in the second version of the schema 'On Ecumenism'.

A consideration of the *modi* of the third session is indispensable, since they are directly necessary for a deeper understanding of the final decree. Here a certain discretion obviously had to be exercised, especially as regards the Council Fathers concerned with the *modi*, but this does not affect the explanation of the texts. In the present book the declarations 'On Religious Liberty' and 'On the Relation of the Church to the non-Christian Religions' have not been discussed. Though both texts are related to the decree 'On Ecumenism', no final decision was reached on them during the third session.

Looking back at the history of this decree I would add a word of thanks to the Secretariat of Christian Unity, its President Cardinal Bea, its Secretary Bishop Johannes Willebrands, the members and *periti* of the Secretariat, and also last but not least to its officials and the others who have worked very devotedly on the suggestions of the Council Fathers to prepare the new texts theologically and 'technically' for the voting. The splendid reward of their hard and selfless labour is the promulgation of the decree 'On Ecumenism', which is not an end but rather a new beginning full of hopes and promises.

Part One

The Origins of the Decree 'On Ecumenism'

1. Progress through the Council

THE FOLLOWING timetable is meant to facilitate a better understanding of the origin and history of the schema 'On Ecumenism':

11 October, 1962	Opening of the Second Vatican Council.
26-29 November, 1962	Discussion of the schema *De Unitate Ecclesiae—ut omnes unum sint*, drawn up by the Commission for the Eastern Churches.
1 December, 1962	The General Congregation of the Council decides on a single schema on ecumenism, in which the schema *De Unitate Ecclesiae* worked out by the Commission for the Eastern Churches is to be combined with the schema *De Oecumenismo* worked out by the Secretariat for Christian Unity and the chapter on ecumenism in the schema *De Ecclesia*.
8 December, 1962	Solemn conclusion of the first session of Vatican II.
January-March, 1963	The Secretariat for Christian Unity works out the first version of the

	schema *De Oecumenismo* in collaboration with the Oriental and Theological Commissions.
22 April, 1963	John XXIII orders the schema *De Oecumenismo* (first version) to be presented to the Council for discussion and to be sent to the Fathers.
May, 1963	The first version is sent to the Fathers of the Council, who during the following months communicate their first comments on the schema to the General Secretariat of the Council.
3 June, 1963	Pope John dies on Whit Monday, at 7.49 p.m.
21 June, 1963	Cardinal Montini is elected Pope and assumes the name Paul VI.
18 August, 1963	In his address at Grottaferrata Paul VI speaks of the Eastern Churches in an ecumenical spirit.
29 September, 1963	Paul VI opens the second session of the Council. In his opening address he speaks at length on ecumenism.
18 November, 1963	Cardinal Cicognani gives the *Introductio* and Archbishop Martin of Rouen the *relatio* on the first version of the schema on ecumenism in the Council hall. Beginning of the general discussion of the schema.

21 November, 1963 — Beginning of the discussion of Chapter One of the schema, 'Principles of Catholic ecumenism', which is dealt with in three General Congregations of 21, 22 and 25 November.

25 November, 1963 — Beginning of the discussion of Chapter Two of the schema, 'The Practical Realization of Ecumenism', carried on in three General Congregations of 25, 26 and 27 November.

27 November, 1963 — Beginning of the discussion of Chapter Three of the schema 'On the Christians Separated from the Catholic Church'. This is dealt with in the General Congregations of 27, 28 and 29 November and concluded on 2 December.

2 December, 1963 — Concluding the discussion of the schema Cardinal Bea asks the Fathers to send in further suggestions for the schema by 31 January, 1964.

4 December, 1963 — Solemn conclusion of the second session of the Council; promulgation of the constitution 'On the Sacred Liturgy' and the decree 'On the Means of Communication'.

4-6 January, 1964 — Pilgrimage of Pope Paul VI to the Holy Land with important ecu-

	menical addresses and events. Meeting between the Pope and Patriarch Athenagoras of Constantinople.
3-24 February, 1964	A committee of Council experts of the Secretariat for Christian Unity, advised by experts of the Oriental and Theological Commissions, sorts out the criticisms and suggestions made by the Council Fathers orally or in writing and makes proposals for their treatment by the Secretariat of Unity.
25 February-7 March, 1964	In a plenary session of the Secretariat for Christian Unity at Ariccia near Rome work on the wishes of the Fathers is completed and the text of the second version of the schema on ecumenism is finished.
27 April, 1964	Paul VI orders the second version of the schema on ecumenism to be presented to the third session of the Council for discussion and to be sent to the Fathers.
May, June, July, 1964	The second version of the schema is sent to the Council Fathers; some of them give their views on the new text in writing.
5 October, 1964	The Council votes with a very large majority in favour of the first four articles of the schema.

6 October, 1964	The vote on the first chapter as a whole results in a large majority for this chapter. The text of Chapter Two is approved in four individual votes on articles 5-6, 7, 8 and 9-12.
7 October, 1964	The Council Fathers approve Chapter Two as a whole with a large majority. They also approve of the texts of Chapter Three in three individual votes on articles 13, 14-18 and 19-24.
8 October, 1964	The Council Fathers approve Chapter Three as a whole with a large majority.
9 October, 1964	The Secretariat for Christian Unity sets up three sub-commissions, which work out proposals for dealing with the additions (*modi*) suggested by the Council Fathers to be submitted to the plenary assembly of the Secretariat.
10 November, 1964	By a large majority the Council Fathers approve the treatment of the additions to Chapter One by the Secretariat for Christian Unity.
11 November, 1964	By a large majority the Council Fathers approve the treatment of the additions to Chapter Two by the Secretariat.

14 November, 1964   By a large majority the Council Fathers approve the treatment of the additions to Chapter Three by the Secretariat.

19 November, 1964   Nineteen alterations of the text are inserted in the schema to produce the final version.

20 November, 1964   The voting on the whole schema *De Oecumenismo* results in a large majority in its favour.

21 November, 1964   The final voting on the schema results in almost unanimous agreement. Pope Paul VI confirms and promulgates the decree *De Oecumenismo* at the solemn conclusion of the third session of the Council.

Congar rightly says that this great and beautiful text is self-explanatory and has a permanent value of its own. 'The decree expresses the mind of John XXIII, who, even though he did not write a single line of it, may be considered its spiritual author. Indeed, John XXIII wanted the Council, and set before it two aims which he saw as very closely related to one another: the inner renewal of the Church and the work of Christian reunion. It was John XXIII who invited the non-Catholic Christian communities to send observers to the Council. While personally welcoming their 'valued presence', he also gave the observers every facility to go about their work in an atmosphere of trust and sincerity. John XXIII created the Secretariat for Unity to receive the observers, to give them every chance to express their opinions, and to discuss with them any questions arising from this ecumenical approach. He entrusted the direction of the Secretariat to Cardinal Bea, assisted by Bishop Willebrands. And finally, it was John XXIII who from the very beginning of the Council gave the Secretariat equal status with the Conciliar Commissions. This was a decision of great moment: it allowed the Secretariat for Unity to intervene in the Council and to submit drafts with the same authority as the Commissions themselves. The present text of the decree must be attributed juridically to this decision, which was truly a sensational one, even though it was couched in very discreet terms.

'The text of the decree "On Ecumenism" has the qualities of an original document, uniform in style and carefully balanced, despite the fact that it is the result of three earlier texts. At the beginning of the first session in the autumn of 1962 the Council was confronted with the following drafts:

a chapter on ecumenism was included in the draft of the Constitution *De Ecclesia* submitted to the Fathers;

a separate draft entitled *De Unitate Ecclesiae—Ut omnes unum sint* was composed by the Commission for Eastern Churches;

a further draft was prepared by the Secretariat of Christian Unity. The Fathers knew only of the existence of this draft, but a considerable number of them expressed their support for it in advance. The other two, which had already been printed and distributed, were submitted and discussed after the schemata on the liturgy and the sources of revelation.'[1]

[1] Yves M.-J. Congar, O.P., *Concile Oecuménique Vatican II, L'Église, L'Oecuménisme, Les Églises Orientales*, Paris, 1965, Introduction, pp. 165-6.

2. Origin and Preparation of the First Version of the Schema

ON 26 NOVEMBER, 1962 the Council began to work on the schema 'On the Unity of the Church—That All May be One'. The text, presented by the Commission for the Eastern Churches, was discussed by three General Congregations on 27, 28 and 29 November. Though the title of the schema suggested that the unity of all Christians would be discussed, it soon emerged from the discussion that only the Eastern Churches were dealt with, and even of these only the ones in full communion with the Apostolic Roman See. The Eastern Churches separated from Rome were mentioned only as far as their relations with the Catholic Eastern Churches were concerned. During the discussion the Fathers acknowledged the positive elements of the schema, but they criticized a certain legalistic outlook and an insufficient regard for the Eastern traditions and the patriarchates.

The Fathers soon realized that the problems of ecumenism would have to be treated within a wider framework and homogeneously; for there cannot be two separate theological conceptions of ecumenism each divided from the other, the one dealing with the relation of the Roman Catholic Church to the Eastern Churches, the other with the ecclesial communities derived from the Reformation.

Ecumenism is closely connected with ecclesiology and derives from this its homogeneous dogmatic foundation and its theological character.

Nevertheless it remains true that the methods and practical applications of ecumenism vary according to different conditions. Thus it was possible for three different drafts on the subject to be submitted at the first session of the Council: apart from the above-mentioned schema of the Commission for Eastern Churches, the original schema *De Ecclesia* contained an eleventh chapter entitled *De Oecumenismo*. This chapter contains valuable material and, after an introduction, is divided into the following sections:

'On the ties already existing and the unity willed by Christ.' 'On the relation of the Catholic Church to individual separated Christians.' 'On the relation of the Catholic Church to the separated Christian communities.' 'On the relation of the Catholic Church to the ecumenical movement outside the Church.' 'On the aim of the ecumenical movement within the Catholic Church and on the dangers to be avoided.' 'On co-operation in sacred liturgical actions.' 'On the collaboration of Catholics with Christians separated from us.'

This brief survey shows that essential problems of ecumenism had already been discussed in this document, which transcended the framework of a dogmatic constitution 'On the Church', however, and came down to practical questions.

The Secretariat for Christian Unity, in its turn, had prepared a schema 'On Ecumenism', because it was realized that this theme required uniform and comprehensive treatment. This schema, however, had not yet been sent to the

Fathers of the Council. Towards the end of the discussion of the schema 'On the Unity of the Church', Cardinal Bea praised its spirit and its good intentions; nevertheless he felt that the time was not ripe for a decision on that document, because ecumenism would have to be considered and discussed as a whole. The presidents of the Council therefore proposed to conclude the debate, and this was agreed by the Fathers.

The following day, 1 December, 1962, the presidents of the General Congregation proposed the following resolution to the vote: 'Having finished the examination of the draft decree on the unity of the Church (*Ut omnes unum sint*), the Fathers approve the draft as a document containing the universal truths of the faith and as a sign of respect and good will towards the separated brethren of the East. In accordance with the remarks and proposals made in the Council hall, however, this decree is to be welded into a single document together with the decree on ecumenism and the chapter on the same subject contained in the schema on the dogmatic constitution of the Church.'

Of the 2112 Fathers present, 2068 voted for and only 36 against this proposal, 8 votes being invalid.

This decision was very important for the further treatment of ecumenism by the Council. A brief section 'On the ties of the Church with the non-Catholic Christians' remained in the new draft of the schema 'On the Church' which had been sent to the Fathers on 22 April, 1963; it was included in the first chapter of this schema and belongs to the ecclesiological foundations of ecumenism. The Commission for the Eastern Churches confined the subject of its draft to those Churches in full communion with Rome; it was chiefly concerned with measures of discipline. The draft, which was approved and sent to the Fathers on 22 April, 1963, is entitled 'De Ecclesiis Orientalibus'. Its first forty-four sections are devoted only to disciplinary questions, while sections 45-54 consider individual problems of relations to the separated Eastern Churches with a view to future unity. It is expressly stated that the general questions are left to the schema 'On Ecumenism'. The differences between the two schemata were clearly emphasized by Coadjutor Archbishop Gabriel Bukatko in his *relatio* of 18 November, 1963.

3. The First Version of the Schema 'On Ecumenism', 22 April, 1963 and the relatio of Archbishop Martin

THE SECRETARIAT for Christian Unity, in conjunction with members of the Theological and the Eastern Churches Commissions worked on the first draft 'On Ecumenism', until spring, 1963. On 22 April Pope John sanctioned it to be submitted to the Council and sent to the Fathers.

This first draft already possesses the structure of the final decree. It comprises three chapters:

 I. 'On the Principles of Catholic Ecumenism.'
 II. 'On the Practical Realization of Ecumenism.'
 III. 'On Christians Separated from the Catholic Church.'

Chapter Three is divided into two parts, 'On the particular position of the Eastern Churches' and 'On the Communities that have originated since the sixteenth century'. The second draft of the schema and the final decree retained this basic structure, though important emendations were made both in form and content and even in the headings of the individual chapters.

The schema 'On Ecumenism' was worked out chiefly by Belgian, French and Dutch theologians. The General Congregations began discussion of it on 18 November,

1963, Cardinal Cicognani giving the general introduction. He is the president of the Commission for the Eastern Churches, which had presented its schema 'On the Unity of the Church' as early as 26 November, 1962 and had had an important share in the schema 'On Ecumenism'. In his introduction Cicognani defended the title, the correct understanding of which had been prepared by utterances of the popes from Leo XIII onwards as well as by the Instruction of the Holy Office 'On the Ecumenical Movement' of 20 December, 1949. The cardinal said further that the title was in accordance with the pastoral aims of the Second Vatican Council and with the universal commission Christ had given to his Church.

After this, Archbishop Martin of Rouen delivered his *relatio* on the schema, which remains important for the understanding of the final decree. He began by stating that the schema was neither a theological manual nor a treatise on canon law, nor even a historical presentation of the subject. In his allocution to the observer delegates of 17 October, 1963 Pope Paul VI had warned against re-opening historical wounds which had not yet completely healed. But this limitation did not mean that theological doctrine, canon law or church history were ignored. On the contrary, all this was presupposed, and also especially the doctrine of the Church, which was being treated in a dogmatic constitution of its own.

Archbishop Martin then went on to speak of the real intention of the schema. Its authors had wanted to prepare a sober pastoral document, penetrated by a sound peaceful spirit, designed to give Catholics a better understanding of the nature, attitude and providential significance of the ecumenical movement. The special emphasis on the novelty of the schema was of particular importance.

Ecumenism, said the archbishop, is something completely new. It has never been dealt with by any previous Council; even in theology it has been discussed only in recent times. It comprises many problems which have not yet received a complete answer. Despite these difficulties the question of ecumenism is of such importance that our Council cannot possibly pass it over in silence. The necessity of treating it results from the new intellectual and spiritual situation of the present day. What then is this particular situation? It is due to the fact that today the centuries-old separation is a real scandal to both Christians and non-Christians. For this separation is against the explicit will of Christ and as it were paralyses the evangelization of the world and the extension of God's kingdom—a fact confirmed by sad everyday experience.

The *relatio* went on to explain the schema in detail. Chapter One describes the unity and uniqueness of the Church of Jesus Christ, the relation of the separated brethren and their communities to the Catholic Church, and the essence of ecumenism.

The archbishop then reported in greater detail on Chapter Two, which aimed at realizing the many suggestions of Pope John XXIII: it is not enough just to talk about ecumenism, and it is even less desirable to regard it as a passing fashion. On the contrary, individual believers as well as Holy Mother Church should use whatever necessary and useful means nature and grace offered to reach the goal of unity. John XXIII and Paul VI, who had faithfully taken over the legacy of his predecessor, had especially emphasized, as the most important of these means, spiritual renewal and humble prayer. Without interior renewal, without the conversion of the heart and a life modelled on Christ, there can be neither a fruitful ecumenism nor that *aggiornamento* which Pope John set in motion and held up as the goal of the Council. Moreover, we need unanimous prayer so that the last wish of Christ, pronounced on the eve of his Passion, may become a new and living reality among us.

To this must be added mutual knowledge and loving understanding, as well as co-operation with the separated brethren 'in works of love, flowing from the spirit of the gospel'. Finally the archbishop spoke of Chapter Three, equally important for both the present and the future. The benevolent attitude to our separated brethren, based on respect and love, had so surprised certain Catholics that someone had even spoken of a panegyric on the heretics. To this the archbishop replied:

It is well known to all the members of the Secretariat for Christian Unity as well as to all observer delegates that there are differences both of doctrine and of ecclesiastical constitution between Catholics and other Christians, as well as mutual historical reproaches, and no one is under any illusion that these are not weighty matters. None of us would be prepared to accept an equivocal or superficial formula of union. There is neither duplicity nor insidiousness nor machiavellism among us. Our relations have been marked from the beginning by sincerity, purity of intention and a research that seeks the truth, desires the light, and above all looks for Jesus in the scriptures.

Since this is explicitly acknowledged by all, it is neither necessary nor useful constantly to repeat all the doctrinal differences well known to us and thus to renew the pain unnecessarily. What is most necessary now is to look for a common basis from which to start the dialogue. This should lead us to consider our actual differences in a new perspective and a more favourable state of mind. This is the reason why the schema mentions doctrinal differences so discreetly.

With regard to the ecumenical dialogue, Archbishop Martin said that of course no truth of the faith would be concealed or minimized in an authentic dialogue whose aim was that all should arrive at a more and more perfect understanding of the Word of God.

Many individual questions could not be treated in this schema but would have to be left to the *Directorium Oecumenicum* which was being prepared by the Secretariat for Unity. Its general rules would have to be adapted by the individual bishops' conferences to the different conditions of the various countries and continents. At the end Archbishop Martin pointed to the theology of history: from the outset the origin of the ecumenical movement had shown the action of the Holy Spirit, as had already been stressed by the Instruction of the Holy Office of 20 December, 1949. If the events that had taken place since then in the Catholic Church, in the World Council of Churches and indeed all over the globe were regarded with the eyes of faith we would see this: in *De Civitate Dei*, St Augustine had described the struggle of the evil spirit against the Holy Spirit in the course of history; in our time this struggle is carried on in quite new circumstances and with new and extremely effective weapons. And in this world are to be found the invitations and impulses of the Holy Spirit, who calls all Christians marked by the indelible seal of baptism to the common search so that all might obtain that unity which the Saviour has implored for the well-being of all mankind and the glorification of God the Father. Perhaps we might even be witnesses of the firstfruits of future unity, the attainment of which is in the hands of God: 'O the depths of the riches and wisdom and knowledge of God! How unsearchable are his judgements and how inscrutable his ways!' (Rom. 11:33).

4. *Discussion of the First Version in the Council Hall. Preparation of a New Version*

THE FIRST draft contained a fourth chapter on the relation of the Church to the Jews and a fifth on religious liberty. At the beginning of the General Congregation of 19 November, 1963, the moderators interrupted the discussion of the day before on the schema in general, asking Cardinal Bea to speak first. His impressive *relatio* on Chapter Four was based on the bible. After him Bishop de Smedt of Bruges delivered his *relatio* on Chapter Five. Then the discussion of the schema as a whole was continued. On 21 November at 11 a.m. the moderators put to the vote the question whether the first three chapters of the schema 'On Ecumenism' should be accepted as a foundation for further discussion. 1970 Council Fathers voted in favour and only 86 against the proposal. Thus the first three chapters, which formed the original subject of the schema, had been accepted by the plenary assembly with a majority of 95·8% as the foundation of their deliberations. This was an extraordinary and unexpected success.

The General Congregations discussed the first chapter from 22 to 25 November, the second from 11.15 a.m. on 25 November till 27 November, and the third from 10.50 a.m.

on 27 November till 2 December. A discussion and vote on
Chapters Four and Five of the schema (relations with the Jews
and 'On religious liberty') were prevented by lack of time.
However, many positions had been made clear in the preceding discussions which were supplemented by written
statements.

At the end of the discussion Cardinal Bea, President of the
Secretariat for Christian Unity, once more addressed the
Council. First he thanked all the Fathers for their valuable
contributions to the discussion of the schema.

> If anyone outside our Church, said the Cardinal, still
> doubted the ecumenical attitude of the Catholic bishops,
> he will now know better. This is proved by the very large
> majority with which the Fathers have accepted the schema
> as a foundation for discussion ... The discussions of these
> last days have shown that all interventions, including
> those which were critical, were inspired by loving desire
> for the unity of Christians. All suggestions and proposals
> will be carefully examined and evaluated by the Secre-
> tariat for Unity, which two months ago appointed sub-
> commissions to study the votes of the Fathers—these are
> already working.

In conclusion, the Cardinal pointed out that the discussions
in the Council hall had shown how much conditions for
ecumenical work varied from country to country. This
made it necessary for the bishops to adapt the general
directives on ecumenism to the special conditions of their
regions.

Indeed, the discussions of the schema had been surprisingly
frank and kept to a high level. A wealth of valuable theo-

logical and practical suggestions and clarifications had been produced, as well as hints for relations with other churches and communions. There was now very valuable material available for the revision of the schema as well as important elements for the further development of the theology of ecumenism. Among these are, for example, the beginnings of a theology dealing with the separation of the Churches; a historico-theological consideration of the Church's path from the Ascension of Christ until his Second Coming; and a more pneumatological view of ecumenism.

The material available for the revision of the schema at the beginning of 1964 contained sixty proposals that had already been submitted before the second session of the Council and 471 contributions which had been submitted by the Fathers either orally or in writing during the second session or after it. The suggestions made before the discussion at the Council already filled 102 pages; those dealing with the schema in general are contained in a volume of 124 pages; those on Chapters One and Two of the schema fill a further volume of 341 pages and those on Chapter Three another one of 144 pages. To this must be added 72 pages on the relations with the Jews and no fewer than 280 pages on religious liberty.

These suggestions arranged in six volumes were sent for study to all the members and special theologians (*periti*) of the Secretariat for Christian Unity. Then a group consisting of *periti* of the Secretariat and delegates from the Eastern churches and Theological Commissions was entrusted with preparing a new text of the schema in accordance with the wishes of the Council Fathers. This was done with great care, and in a plenary session of the Secretariat presided over by Cardinal Bea, which took place from 24 February to 7

March in the Casa Gesù Divin Maestro at Ariccia near Rome, the new version was thoroughly discussed and its final form almost unanimously accepted. On 27 April, 1964, Pope Paul VI ordered this version to be submitted to the third session; it was consequently sent to the Council Fathers and is the actual model for the final decree, hardly having been changed during the third session.

These are the principles according to which the texts accepted on 21 November, 1963 as the basis for the discussions had been drawn up:

1. The structure and statements of the original text were altered only if the Council Fathers had explicitly demanded it.

2. If the alterations suggested by the Fathers appeared to be necessary or at least useful for an improvement or a better understanding of the text, then longer sections were changed.

3. If the wishes of the Fathers could be met by minor alterations or additions, this was done even if the change was not really necessary.

4. Some proposals could not be accepted because they were either incompatible with the content and the pastoral outlook of the schema or because they belonged to the *Directorium Oecumenicum* to be compiled by the Secretariat.

This second version of the schema is the direct predecessor of the final decree and did not undergo any essential alterations. This is shown by the following survey of its contents which explains the intentions of the schema. The headings accompanying the numbers of the schema were left out in the final decree.

5. *The Second Version of the Schema, 27 April, 1964*

THE TITLE

THE TITLE 'On Ecumenism' has been retained. In the romance and English-speaking countries it has already become a technical term, though this decree will probably mostly be quoted by its initial words *Unitatis redintegratio*, 'The Restoration of Unity'.

THE DIVISIONS

The new version has retained the structure of the first three chapters. The chapter 'On Religious Liberty' was added as Chapter Four. According to a frequently voiced wish of the Council Fathers the former Chapter Four on the relation to the Jews was added to the schema as an Appendix. The new schema is divided as follows:

Chapter One	On the Catholic principles of ecumenism
Chapter Two	On the practical realization of ecumenism
Chapter Three	On the churches and ecclesial communities separated from the Apostolic See of Rome
Part I	On the Special consideration of the Eastern Churches

Article 1: The Introduction

The following are the main ideas of the Introduction which sound some of the keynotes of the whole schema:

1. The fact that Christendom is divided and the scandal of these divisions which are opposed to the will of Christ. The schema 'On Ecumenism' does not present a 'theology of ecclesial separations', though the discussions of the second session of the Council furnished important elements for this. Several Fathers pointed out the share which on both sides sin and guilt had in these divisions, which will always remain a mystery to Christians.

2. The separated brethren's desire for ecclesial unity. In this section the origin and merits of the ecumenical movement are emphasized in accordance with the wishes of many Council Fathers. The basic formula of the World Council of Churches is mentioned as well as the goal of an all-embracing visible ecclesial unity.

3. After a mention of the doctrine on the Church already declared by the Council, which is presupposed in the schema, the introduction explains the purpose of the whole schema: it will show Catholics in what way they can help make the desire for unity among Christians more effective.

Thus the aim is limited. The schema does not intend to draw up an ecumenical programme for all Christendom, nor is it a manifesto of union or an invitation to non-Catholic Christians. It is rather a pastoral directive intended to encourage and prepare ecumenical thought and action in the Catholic Church. For this reason the schema 'On Ecumenism' has the form of a decree, while the schema on the Church is presented as a Dogmatic Constitution. Moreover, this decree is the practical application of what the Constitution had said about the Church, about the mystery of the pilgrim people of God, which lives by the unique event that is Christ. Under the guidance of God's grace and his incomprehensible judgements, this Church is on its way to meet the returning Christ in much tribulation, temptation and failure, always open to the action of the Holy Spirit by which it lives, always ready to listen to the call of the Lord. In the schema on the Church the ecumenical dimension is already implicit; it is unfolded in the schema 'On Ecumenism'.[1]

CHAPTER ONE: ON THE CATHOLIC PRINCIPLES OF ECUMENISM

In the first draft the title of this chapter had been 'On the Principles of Catholic Ecumenism'. The alteration was demanded by several Fathers and is justified, for strictly speaking there can hardly be Catholic ecumenism, but rather Catholic principles of ecumenism. For the 'ecumenical movement' in the narrower sense of the word originated about the beginning of this century outside the Catholic Church. The Catholic Church shares in the movement according to its own principles. It is noteworthy that the World Council of Churches does not impose an ecclesiology of its own and

[1] Cf. J. Ratzinger, 'Die Kirche und die Kirchen', in *Reformatio* 1964, 2, pp. 97 f.

that all its member churches retain their own ecclesiological principles. Even more will the Catholic Church, which is not a member, participate according to its own principles in the universal ecumenical movement.

The new title also avoids the appearance of wanting to form a 'Catholic' ecumenical block, comprising the Orthodox, as opposed to a 'Protestant' ecumenism.[1]

Several Fathers had wanted the concept of ecumenism to be presented more clearly, others demanded a description that would avoid scholastic formulae. But as ecumenism is a movement for advancing the unity of all Christians in the one Church of Jesus Christ, it cannot be defined scholastically according to genus and species. On the other hand it can be described as is done in Article 3 of the schema. This explanation comprises a description of the general ecumenical movement and its specific application to Catholics.

Article 2: 'The unity and uniqueness of the Church'

Several Fathers had demanded a more explicit dogmatic foundation of the schema. The new text observes the following rules relevant to this question:

1. As has been said in the Introduction, the scheme presupposes the dogmatic teaching of the constitution 'De Ecclesia'.

---

[1] Cf. R. Laurentin, *L'enjeu du Concile. Bilan de la Deuxième Session.* Paris, Editions du Seuil, 1964, p. 163: 'Must we speak of a Catholic ecumenism? Is not this a somewhat hasty position which risks leading to the formation of two ecumenical blocks? Should not the schema be quite consciously more empirical, as befits a simple Decree? Therefore should not the title of the first chapter be changed into "Catholic Principles of Ecumenism"...'

2. Some theological propositions have been added explaining the unity which Christ has given to his Church. This doctrine is presented rather summarily; in greater detail it must be understood within the context of the full Catholic teaching as expressed in the doctrinal utterances of the Church.

3. For clarity's sake the following elements have been given greater emphasis:

(a) Christ founded his one unique Church for this present age of the world. Her unity is not a dimension meant to take shape only in the future or at the Second Coming of Christ.

(b) Christ entrusted the office of teaching, guiding and sanctifying to the college of apostles.

(c) He founded his Church on Peter, to whom he gave the keys of the kingdom of heaven and the office of guarding all in the perfect unity of the Church.

(d) Nevertheless, Christ himself remains for ever the corner stone of the whole edifice of the Church.

(e) The presentation closely follows the scriptures. It does not decide certain questions on which exegetes differ: a question, for example, such as the exact date of Peter's election as the head of the apostolic college.

4. The importance of the eucharist for the unity of the Church and the working of the Holy Spirit as the invisible principle of this unity are stated more clearly than in the first draft. This had been the wish of several Fathers.

Article 3: '*The relation of the separated brethren to the Catholic Church*'

Concerning the relation of the separated churches and communions to the one and unique Church of Christ, several Fathers had said that the separated communions because of their separation could not be means of sanctification.

In the schema it is stated that the Holy Spirit does not refuse to use them as means of salvation. It goes on to say that their power derives from the fullness entrusted to the Church. The schema says further that the means of salvation that have remained in the separated communions belong to the one Church of Christ, and hence not to the communions insofar as they are separated. It cannot, however, be denied that these communions possess elements through which the unity of the Church is *also* made manifest. This is especially evident in the Orthodox celebration of the eucharist.

The schema does not hide the fact that in part there are very serious obstacles with regard to doctrine, church order and the structure of the Church which prevent full ecclesial communion.

The following subjects are explained more fully than in the first draft of the schema.

1. The renewal of the Church through penance and confession of guilt.

2. The imperfections and flaws of the Church insofar as it is a human community.

3. Unity in diversity and justified pluralism (in articles 3 and 4 of the schema).

4. The catholicity of the Church (in articles 3 and 4).

The following elements are briefly introduced or suggested:

1. The missionary element in ecumenism, briefly mentioned in the Introduction.

2. The dynamism of salvation history: though in its earthly pilgrimage the people of God remains tainted by sin, it nevertheless grows constantly in Christ and is graciously guided by God according to his mysterious counsels until it reaches the fullness of the eternal glory in the heavenly Jerusalem.

3. The commandment of love towards the separated Christians.

4. The separations within Christendom are unnatural and are opposed to the will of Christ.

5. The dynamic character of ecumenism is emphasized in article 4.

6. The schema speaks frequently of 'the brethren separated from us' in order to indicate that the separation is mutual.

7. The suggestions of the Fathers contain the beginnings of a 'theology of the separation of the churches', but its elaboration would go beyond the scope of the present schema. The text says only that in the one and only Church of Christ 'certain divisions have sprung up, which the apostle (1 Cor. 1:11; 11:22) gravely reprimands as to be condemned'. Instead of the former 'schisms' (*schismata*), a word which has acquired a special technical sense, the schema uses the equally scriptural term 'divisions' (*scissurae*), which better expresses the meaning of this passage. The evil contained in every division is specially emphasized.

The schema says further: 'Communities of considerable

size have broken away from full fellowship in the Catholic Church. The fault has sometimes been on both sides.' Though the sins of the Church do not justify the separation, it must nevertheless be admitted that they have furthered the divisions. The schema states explicitly that the Christians now living within the separated communions are not guilty of the separation and are treated by the Catholic Church with reverent brotherly love. 'Baptized believers in Christ have a certain, even though still imperfect, communion with the Catholic Church.' This proposition is based on sound theological principles; it is also supported by the allocutions of Pope Paul VI at Grottaferrata and at Bethlehem. On the other hand, the schema does not fail to point out the deep doctrinal, liturgical and constitutional differences which the ecumenical movement has to overcome.

Article 4: 'Ecumenism'

The article begins with a descriptive explanation of ecumenism, followed by a further exposition of some of its elements, such as better mutual knowledge, dialogue, mutual esteem, collaboration, renewal according to the will of Christ, the goal of unity which Christ gave to his Church from the beginning. True, this unity cannot be lost and is always present in the Catholic Church, but it is capable of growth until the end of time.

Some of the Fathers' suggestions showed uncertainty about the relation of ecumenism to conversions and their preparation; here a brief paragraph has been inserted into the schema: there is no opposition between the two, even though they differ both in their end and in their method.

The schema further demands the renewal of the Church through the gospel; it gives reasons for the diversities in unity, in the theological presentation of revealed truth as well as in the liturgy and in spirituality. The faithful are asked to recognize the riches of Christ and the gifts of the Spirit possessed by the separated brethren, especially as they sometimes bear witness to Christ even to laying down their life.

Should the separations be overcome, the 'plenitude of catholicity' would become more effective and be more fully expressed in the life of the Church.

CHAPTER TWO: 'THE PRACTICAL REALIZATION OF ECUMENISM'

Article 5 of the schema says first of all that the very desire to restore unity bears witness to a brotherly relationship among all Christians and is meant to lead to perfect unity according to God's gracious will.

Article 6: 'The renewal of the Church'

Many bishops had asked that the schema should not only mention the Christian renewal of individual persons but also the reform of the whole Church with regard to the cure of souls, the institutions of human law and also the theological presentation (of the faith). Hence the schema says: 'The pilgrim Church is called by Christ to that constant reform which it always needs insofar as it is a human and earthly institution.'

Article 7: 'The conversion of the heart'

In this section something is said about confession of guilt concerning the divisions, in connection with 1 John 1:10.

We ask God and our separated brethren for forgiveness, as we, too, forgive them that trespass against us.

Article 8: 'Unanimous prayer'

Prayer for the unity of Christians is called the soul of the whole ecumenical movement. The earlier text, which dealt with the *communicatio in sacris*, had been vigorously criticized, especially by the Eastern Fathers. They demanded that the possibility of a far-reaching *communicatio* with the Orthodox should be left open. In the East, they said, there was no danger of indifferentism, while the refusal of the *communicatio* was felt to be a grave scandal.

The schema gives two general principles of the *communicatio in sacris* but leaves its practical application to later legislation and to the pastoral prudence of the bishops. These two principles are, first, the *communicatio in sacris* symbolizes the unity of the Church. For this reason it is frequently not possible to practise it because there is not sufficient unity. Secondly, *communicatio in sacris* means sharing in the means of grace. On these grounds it is in some cases possible. For it should be remembered that the Orthodox have preserved the apostolic succession of the bishops as well as the valid celebration of the eucharist, as is explicitly stated in Part One of Chapter Three.

Article 9: 'The mutual knowledge of the brethren'

This section recommends the better knowledge of the doctrine and history, the spirituality, the worship and the psychology of the separated brethren. Theological conferences of experts should be arranged under the supervision of the bishops to discuss matters as equals.

Article 10: 'Ecumenical instruction'

All theology and especially Church history should be taught in the ecumenical spirit, so that the presentation may be more in accordance with historical truth. The expression *rerum veritati* means historical truth, not dogma. Future priests are to be sufficiently instructed in ecumenical problems, so that they can teach the faithful also. It is pointed out that such instruction is particularly necessary in the missions.

Article 11: 'The manner in which the doctrine of the faith is expressed and presented'

This treats of the most important condition for the dialogue with our separated brethren. The whole of Catholic doctrine is to be presented clearly and without omissions. The methods and expressions of a more profound and exact explanation are to be suited to the understanding of the separated brethren. Those taking part in the dialogue will compete in a brotherly manner to combine love of the truth with humble charity.

Article 12: 'Collaboration with the separated brethren'

According to a wish expressed in the Council hall, this section begins with the witness of a common faith in the Trinity, the incarnation and the redemption. All true Christians should bear witness to this in mutual esteem and in the hope of eternal life. This mutual respect is especially set in opposition to the false proselytism of which particularly the Latin American bishops had complained. This is followed by a recommendation to work with others in the causes of world peace, social justice, scientific progress, scholarship, art and civilization.

Many Fathers had expressed the wish that the common service of Christians should be modelled on the suffering servant of Isaiah. Hence the words of the schema: 'The co-operation of all Christians . . . illuminates the face of Christ the servant.'

CHAPTER THREE: 'ON THE CHURCHES AND ECCLESIAL COMMUNITIES SEPARATED FROM THE APOSTOLIC ROMAN SEE'

The wish had been expressed in the Council hall that a general criterion for the lack of unity should be given in the title of this chapter. Hence communion with the Apostolic Roman See is mentioned here as a criterion of unity and separation; but theological questions are not discussed.

Article 13: Preface

This article explains the order of the whole chapter.

1. There are two great divisions of the Church. The first developed in the East, gradually and at different periods; finally it resulted in the breaking off of communion between the Eastern patriarchates and the Apostolic Roman See. The second originated in the West, in the sixteenth century; it resulted in national and denominational ecclesial communities separated from the Apostolic Roman See.

2. These two divisions are very different from each other, both with regard to questions of faith and to the structure

of the Church. The Council recognizes this difference as well as the ecumenical task common to both divisions. Part One of Chapter Three comprises articles 14-18 under the following headings:

'On the special attitude and history of the Easterns';
'On the liturgical and spiritual tradition of the Easterns';
'On the special discipline of the Easterns';
'On the special way of the Easterns in dealing with divine doctrine.'

Part Two comprises articles 19-24 and deals with the particular situation especially of the reformed ecclesial communities, of their confession of Christ, their relation to Holy Scripture, their sacramental life and their spirituality.

Chapter Three, Part One: 'Special Consideration of the Eastern Churches'

In his *relatio* of 18 November, 1963 on this first part, Coadjutor-Archbishop Gabriel Bukatko had set out the difference between the schema 'On the Eastern Churches' and that 'On Ecumenism'. The latter deals in general with the relation of the Eastern Churches separated from Rome with the Roman Catholic Church, while the schema on the Eastern Churches treats of the special relation of the Eastern Catholic Churches united to Rome with their separated Eastern brethren. Hence both schemata have a different purpose.

The following suggestions had been made by the bishops in the Council hall:

1. Explicit mention was to be made of the valid apostolic succession of the Eastern bishops separated from us, the valid

priesthood in these Churches and the preservation of all the sacraments.[1]

2. The importance of the eucharist for the building up of the Church ought to be emphasized. The eucharist is not only a quantitative element added to the others, but a qualitative note of the individual church.

3. The legitimate difference in the special canon law and the hierarchical structures proper to the Eastern Churches should be emphasized more clearly.

4. The plurality of the Eastern Churches with their different traditions should be considered.

5. The steadfastness of the Eastern Churches in many persecutions deserves special praise.

6. It should be emphasized even more strongly that there is no opposition between true catholicity and genuine 'orientality'.

7. The external causes of the separation should at least be suggested without passing judgement on the historical events. But lack of mutual understanding and brotherly love as well as guilt on both sides should humbly be admitted.

These wishes of the bishops have been taken into account in the new version. Part One of Chapter Three, which deals with the Eastern Churches, is now divided as follows:

Article 14: 'The attitude and history proper to the Easterns'

(*a*) The spiritual situation at the time when East and West were united.

(*b*) The origin of the separation.

---

[1] Doubts were expressed about the preservation of *all* the sacraments among the Nestorians (particularly about the anointing of the sick).

Different traditions and the different mentalities 'occasioned' the separation. This means that the separation was by no means a necessary consequence of these occasions.

(c) The importance of a more exact knowledge of these circumstances and of relations between the Eastern Churches and the Apostolic Roman See before the division.

(d) The value of this knowledge and of respect for the Eastern traditions for future unity.

Article 15: 'The liturgical and spiritual tradition of the Easterns'

The liturgical and the spiritual tradition.

The Eastern liturgy.

The celebration of the eucharist and its importance for building up an individual church.

The meaning of concelebration.

The liturgical veneration of the Mother of God and the saints.

The possibility and significance of the *communicatio in sacris* in certain circumstances.

The monastic life and its influence on Western monasticism.

The importance of the liturgical and monastic life for a future unity of the Eastern and Western Churches.

Article 16: 'The special discipline of the Easterns'

Existence and confirmation of these rights.

Their positive influence on the life of the Church.

The right of the Easterns to live according to their own canon law.

The importance of this principle for future unity.

Article 17: 'The special way of the Easterns in dealing with divine doctrine'

A difference in the theological expression of doctrine is legitimate.

The positive aspect of this difference.

The sources of the presentation of Eastern theology.

The value of this tradition.

This whole inheritance of the Easterns belongs to the full catholicity and apostolicity of the Church.

The Catholic Churches of the East united with the Apostolic Roman See wish to preserve this inheritance and to develop it still more perfectly.

Article 18: 'Conclusion and exhortation of the Council'

(a) In order to restore unity nothing should be imposed that is not absolutely necessary (Acts 15:28).

(b) Mutual rapprochement should be prompted, and the dialogue about theological and pastoral questions is important.

(c) Eastern Christians living outside their own territory are recommended to the loving care of the Catholic cure of souls.

(d) The Council hopes that the barrier between the Western and the Eastern Church will one day come down.

CHAPTER THREE, PART TWO: 'THE SEPARATED CHURCHES AND ECCLESIAL COMMUNITIES OF THE WEST'

The original title referred only to those separated communities that have originated since the sixteenth century.

But several Fathers pointed out that this title should comprise not only the reformed communities but also the much earlier Waldensians and the later Old Catholics. Moreover, it was almost impossible not to make a distinction between the Anglicans and all the other reformed communities. Just as the term 'Church' was applied in the dogmatic sense to the separated Eastern Churches, so it should also be applied in an analogous sense to the reformed communities. Cardinal König proposed to use the general term 'ecclesial communities'. Hence the new title has: 'Churches and ecclesial communities.' There are in the West separated communities to which the term 'Church' should be applied in a way similar to the Eastern Churches: for example, the Old Catholic Churches. But there are also communities, for example the Congregationalists, which reject the term 'Church'. The new formulation of the title ought to correspond to the expectations expressed by the Council.

The dogmatic constitution *De Ecclesia* uses the same term in a slightly different Latin form when treating of 'ecclesiastical communities' in article 15, a term that corresponds to the 'ecclesial communities' of the decree 'On Ecumenism'. In the first draft of this decree it had been attempted to reduce the theological opposition of the reformed communities to the Catholic Church to the ultimate principle of overemphasis on the transcendence of God, from which resulted the particular stress on the doctrine of justification and the denial of the essential mediation of the Church.

Many Fathers criticized this attempt. They stressed that it was not the task of the Council to describe the separated communities. Since the Western ecclesial communities separated from the Apostolic Roman See differed from each other such a description could easily lead to inadmissible simplifications. The original division of the section on the separated ecclesial communities in the West is retained in the new version which, after a brief survey of their relation to the Catholic Church, treats of their confession of Christ, their love of holy scripture, their sacramental life and their spirituality. In each case the elements they have in common with the Catholic Church are considered first, because they could be starting points for an ecumenical dialogue. After that the doctrinal differences are briefly indicated; these would have to be the subject of the dialogue.

Article 19: 'The special situation of these communities'

The beginnings of the division of the Western Church are placed at the end of the Middle Ages; thus it takes in the forerunners of the Reformation such as Wycliffe and Hus, as well as the Waldensian movement. The reformed and the other separated Western communities are said to be especially related to the Catholic Church on account of their long history in common. The schema deliberately refrains from stating one ultimate principle of the Western division. Beyond this it is said that on account of the great differences of these separated communities it would be extremely difficult to describe them accurately, nor was this the intention of the Council. But it should be admitted that there are great differences between these churches and communities on the one hand and the Catholic Church on the other. These are not only historical, sociological, psychological and cultural, but concern above all the interpretation of revealed truth. 'But in order that the ecumenical dialogue may be carried on easily, despite these differences, we would now make some statements that could and should provide the foundation and suggestions for this dialogue.'

Thus the intention of the paragraphs which follow is clearly expressed. The aim is not to describe the separated communities but to point out the elements they have in common with the Catholic Church. So as to exclude an easy optimism, the existing doctrinal differences are mentioned in each paragraph after the common elements have been enumerated.

The desire for a special mention of the Anglicans had already been met under article 13 in the Introduction to Chapter Three.

Article 20: 'The confession of Christ'

This section alludes to the basic declaration of the World Council of Churches, but it is reproduced in biblical terminology with a strongly christological element. Its differences from Catholic doctrine on the incarnation, the redemption, the office of the Church and the position of Mary in the plan of salvation are expressly pointed out. The wish of some Fathers to name Christ as the bond uniting all the elements we have in common has been met.

Article 21: 'The study of holy scripture'

This section treats of God's revelation through the incarnate Word and of the consideration of the mysteries of Christ in holy scripture which is the common heritage of

Christendom, as well as of the authority and exploration of the bible as the foundation of the dialogue.

The article clearly points out the different views of the relation of scripture to the Church and its teaching office.

Article 22: 'The sacramental life'

The first draft of the schema was entitled 'On the sacrament of baptism'. The alteration of the title is significant; the sacramental life should be treated as a whole. This was in accordance with the wish of some Fathers and also of some observers.

Where baptism is validly administered and received with due dispositions a man is incorporated into the crucified and glorified Christ and reborn to the divine life. Thus baptism is a sacramental bond of unity between all who are thus reborn. Nevertheless baptism is only the beginning of complete unity. Hence this basic sacrament tends to incorporate men into the full unity of the Church which Christ desired and which is most strongly expressed in the eucharistic communion.

Article 23: 'Life in Christ'

The scriptural spirituality of many separated Christians is praised as much as their charitable and social activities and their work for world peace.

Despite the 'high esteem of baptism' the first version of the schema had mentioned also those 'who do not preserve the reality of this sacrament, but confess that they belong to Christ, love him, lead a spiritual life nourished by the scriptures and assiduously practise the works of charity'. This envisaged Christian communities like the Society of Friends (Quakers) and the Salvation Army. This section did not please all the Fathers. Some asked who was meant by it and where one should draw the line, whether perhaps the Pentecostal sect, too, belonged to this category. Other Fathers felt that one ought not to judge particular Protestant communities. Hence this section has been left out from the second version of the schema.

The different ways of applying the teaching of the gospels to ethical and sociological questions are mentioned and recommended as objects of ecumenical dialogue.

Article 24: Conclusion

The conclusion refers to all three preceding chapters. It is an exhortation to the faithful, stressing particularly that the restoration of the perfect unity of Christians transcends all human powers and gifts and can only be implored humbly and hopefully from the power of the Holy Spirit.

6. The Voting on the Second Version and its Promulgation

THE SECOND version of the first three chapters of the schema needed no further discussion in the third session since it had already been thoroughly debated during the second session. The Fathers had next to vote on the details of the first three chapters and their sub-sections. The voting was preceded by a *relatio* of Archbishop Martin of Rouen on 5 October, 1964, who enlarged on the new version of Chapter One. In particular, he explained the Introduction on the intention of the schema which had been absent from the first version, and spoke further about the stronger emphasis on the working of the Holy Spirit in the history of salvation, on the importance of the change in the title of Chapter One and on the more detailed description of ecumenism. He stressed that those responsible for the new version were well aware of the difficulties in the way of the desired unity of all Christians. The schema certainly did not claim to remove these obstacles but, in accordance with Pope Paul VI's encyclical *Ecclesiam suam*, it pointed out those elements that are common to the various Christian denominations and would facilitate the ecumenical dialogue. The votes were taken after the *relatio* with the following results:

1. On the Introduction (*Prooemium*): 2111 voted: 2094

in favour (*placet*), 16 against (*non placet*), 1 invalid.

2. On article 2, 'Unity and uniqueness of the Church': 2112 voted: 2081 in favour, 30 against, 2 invalid.

3. On article 3, 'The relation of the separated brethren to the Catholic Church': 2110 voted: 2051 in favour, 57 against, 2 invalid.

4. On article 4, 'Ecumenism': 2107 voted: 2056 in favour, 50 against, 1 invalid.

At the beginning of the 95th General Congregation of the Council, on 6 October, 1964, Bishop Charles Helmsing of Kansas City gave the *relatio* on Chapter Two of the schema. After the ecumenical movement and its relation to the Catholic Church had been discussed in general in the first chapter, Chapter Two was concerned with the practical realization of ecumenism among Catholic Christians. The desire for unity strains after the renewal of the Church as it is described in articles 5 and 6 of the schema. The call to a change of heart and the following of Christ is treated in article 7, while article 8 offers an important principle for the *communicatio in sacris* which consists of two, as it were, dialectical parts. The following sections of this chapter concern ways and means towards a better mutual knowledge among the separated brethren.

5. When voting on the chapter as a whole, the Fathers could vote not only *placet* or *non placet* but also *placet iuxta modum* (in favour, but with reservations). The result was: 2166 voted: of these 1926 in favour, 30 against, 209 in favour with reservations, 1 invalid.

There followed the voting on individual parts of Chapter Two.

6. On article 5 'The care for unity is the object of the whole Church' and simultaneously on article 6, 'The renewal of the Church': 2166 voted: 2120 in favour, 46 against.

7. On article 7, 'The conversion of the heart': 2168 voted: 2076 in favour, 92 against.

8. On article 8, 'Unanimous prayer' (with the principles of *communicatio in sacris*): 2166 voted: of these 1872 in favour, 292 against, 2 invalid.

9. On articles 9 'The mutual knowledge of the brethren', 10 'Ecumenical instruction', 11 'The manner in which the doctrine of the faith is expressed and presented', and 12 'Collaboration with the separated brethren': 2161 voted: 2099 in favour, 62 against.

At the beginning of the 96th General Congregation on 7 October, 1964, Archbishop Maximos Hermaniuk of Winnipeg for the Ukrainians in Canada delivered the *relatio* on part one of Chapter Three of the schema, which deals with the Eastern Churches. He emphasized that the separation of the Eastern Church, which began with the unfortunate events of 1044, had not been brought about by doctrinal causes. All should realize that despite their painful separation East and West often differ only in their expressions of the same truth of the faith. Quarrels, mutual accusations and condemnations do great harm to the life of the whole Church. Thus in A.D. 1054 the papal legate Cardinal Humber had groundlessly accused the Patriarch Michael Caerularius and his followers of all the heresies known at the time, and almost three months after the death of Pope Leo IX he had placed the bull of excommunication on the altar of Sancta Sophia at Constantinople. Present historians are convinced that at that time no truths of the faith had been doubted. The present schema was meant to put before the eyes of all Christians the Eastern Churches' special intellectual attitude, history, liturgical tradition, spirituality, theological method and presentation as well as their particular canon law.

Archbishop (now Cardinal) John Heenan then delivered the *relatio* on the second part of Chapter Three, 'On the separated churches and communities of the West'. He made an important remark on the title: 'The Western communities separated from the Apostolic Roman See are not only a sum of individual Christians, but they show church-forming elements which they have preserved from the common inheritance and which give them a truly ecclesial character. If the title of this part speaks of churches and ecclesial communities this is meant to comprise all Christian communities without its being claimed that the controversial question under what conditions a Christian community could be called a church in the theological sense is solved.'

Archbishop Heenan said further that the schema did not want to give a description of these communities. In four sections it presented the elements common to all believers in Christ as well as the distinctive doctrines. This should nullify the warnings of those Fathers who had feared either an inclination to proselytize or dangers of indifferentism. Concluding, Archbishop Heenan pointed out that John XXIII and Paul VI had given the Council a pastoral as well as an ecumenical direction. The schema 'On Ecumenism' would give Catholic priests and faithful the necessary directives and lead to co-operation with our still separated brethren, who are, nevertheless, closely united to us in prayer and Christian hope.

10. In the same General Congregation Chapter Two was voted on as a whole, again with votes of *placet iuxta modum*. The result was as follows: 2174 voted: 1573 in favour, 32 against, 564 in favour with reservations, 5 invalid.

11. Then followed the voting on the individual parts of Chapter Three, and first on the Preface to the whole chapter (article 13): 2177 voted: 2154 in favour, 21 against, 2 invalid.

12. On Part One of Chapter Three, that is, on articles 14, 'The special attitude and history of the Easterns', 15, 'The liturgical and spiritual tradition of the Easterns', 16, 'The special discipline of the Easterns', 17, 'The special way of the Easterns in dealing with divine doctrine' and article 18 with the conclusion of this first part: 2162 voted: 2119 in favour, 39 against, 4 invalid.

13. On Part Two of Chapter Three, 'The separated churches and ecclesial communities of the West', articles 19, 'The special situation of these communities', 20, 'The confession of Christ', 21, 'The study of holy scripture', 22, 'The sacramental life', 23, 'Life in Christ', and 24 with the conclusion of the whole schema: 2133 voted: 2088 in favour, 43 against, 2 invalid.

14. The fourteenth and last partial vote on the schema referred to the whole of Chapter Three. It took place at the 97th General Congregation on 8 October, 1964 with the following results: 2169 voted: 1843 in favour, 24 against, 296 in favour with reservations, 6 invalid.

The votes had resulted in an overwhelming majority for this second version of the schema. True, a considerable minority had agreed to the individual chapters only with reservations. On the first chapter 209 Fathers had voted *placet iuxta modum*, on the second 564 and on the third 296. This meant altogether 1069 votes *iuxta modum*. These reservations or suggestions for alterations were delivered in writing to the general secretariat of the Council on the day of voting or on the following day. Since some Fathers made several proposals for a chapter, this resulted in almost 2000 *modi* or suggestions for alterations for the three chapters of the schema.

The *placet iuxta modum* is usually translated as agreeing with reservations; however, the written additions (*modi*) are only partly genuine reservations, rejecting a certain section, a sentence or even only a word. In many cases the *modus* only recommends an alteration which the Council Father considers an improvement, without wanting to make his assent to the whole chapter dependent on this alteration. This is proved by the votes on the individual sections of the chapter as well as by the final ones on the decree as a whole.

The General Secretariat of the Council turned over all these *modi* to the Secretariat for Christian Unity. This secretariat formed four sub-committees for the first, the second, and Part One and Part Two of the third chapter respectively. These sub-committees began work on the *modi* at once, each one of them, together with the reason given for it, being carefully examined. The sub-committee worked out a recommendation of acceptance or rejection of each *modus*, and in his *relatio* the spokesman of the sub-committee communicated the result to the plenary meeting of the secretariat for unity. Those members of the secretariat who had a vote, all of them Fathers of the Council, decided by vote on the recommendations of the sub-committees. Here, too, the principle followed was that the text accepted by the majority should normally be altered only if the changes suggested were well-founded and accorded with the general content and outlook of the accepted text. There was no obligation to accept the reservations or suggested changes, because the text had been accepted by a two-thirds majority, though this did not prevent each suggestion from being carefully examined.

Thirteen changes in all were made in the Introduction and Chapter One, five in Chapter Two and eleven in Chapter Three. None of the twenty-nine emendations actually changed the content or spirit of the schema; rather they clarified it and prevented misunderstandings.

The results of the work of the Secretariat for Unity were presented to the Council Fathers and the other members in three printed volumes comprising a hundred pages altogether. Each of the three volumes contained all the *modi* for one chapter together with the reasons for them as well as the acceptance or rejection of the *modus* by the Secretariat for Unity together with its reasons.

The General Congregation responded with three ballots on the question whether the Fathers agreed to the examination or treatment of the *modi* on the first, second and third chapters by the Secretariat for Unity. On 10 November, 1964 of the 2119 Fathers voting on Chapter One, 2068 answered this question in the affirmative, 47 in the negative, and 4 votes were invalid. On 11 November, 1964 the same question about Chapter Two was answered by 2109 Fathers, 2021 in favour, 85 against, while 3 votes were invalid. On 14 November, 1964, the same question about

Chapter Three was answered by 1963 Fathers, 1870 in favour, 82 against, 11 invalid. Thus the Council had signified its agreement to the treatment of the *modi* by the Secretariat for Unity with an overwhelming majority.

Only now could the Secretariat for Unity deliver the new text with the accepted additions to the General Secretariat of the Council to be sent on to the Vatican Printing Office. This is the reason why the printing of the schema, which in its entirety had still to be put to the vote of the General Congregations, could take place only shortly before the end of the Third Session of the Council. In the last two weeks, however, the Vatican printers were completely overworked. Neither overtime nor day and night shifts could quite cope with the back-log. These technical obstacles and the ensuing difficulties about keeping to pre-arranged dates were partly responsible for some of the difficulties and measures taken during the last week of this session of the Council.

The outcome shows that a group of the Fathers were not in agreement with the *expensio modorum*. The votes against the treatment of the *modi* to Chapters 2 and 3 were 85 and 83 respectively. This small minority believed that insufficient attention had been paid to their objections. By the way things were going in the Council these Fathers thought that a petition to the pope was the only way to obtain a further hearing for their persistent misgivings. If comparison is made of the *modi* rejected by the Secretariat for Unity with the alterations inserted on 19 November it will be seen that several of the rejected *modi* correspond to the final corrections; this is clear from the following conspectus:

Text of the schema of 27 April, 1964	*Rejected modi*	*Alterations to text of 19 November, 1964*
Article 3 quae Ecclesiae con- credita est	dicatur: quae 'uni' Ecclesiae concredita est	quae Ecclesiae 'catholicae' con- credita est
Article 4 Spiritu Sancto afflante	dicatur: afflante quidem Spiritus Sancti gratia	afflante Spiritus Sancti gratia
Article 16 memores necessariae unitatis totius Ec- clesiae jus et officium habere	vox 'officium' expungatur	totius Ecclesiae 'facultatem' habere
Article 17 variae illae theolo- gicae formulae potius inter se compleri	variae illae theologicae formulae saepe saepius potius inter se compleri	formulae non raro potius inter se compleri
Article 21 Spiritu Sancto movente	deleantur verba: Spiritu Sancto movente	Spiritum Sanctum invocantes
in ipsis Sacris Scripturis Deum inveniunt	loco inveniunt dicatur: quaerunt	in ipsis Sacris Scripturis Deum inquirunt
Article 22 plenam realitatem Eucharistiae non servaverint	deleatur verbum plenam; loco plenam dicatur veram	genuinam atque inte- gram substantiam Mysterii Eucharistici

The reasons for the suggested alterations are very revealing, and these will be set out below in the detailed explanation of the articles. Mention should be made here of a further fact: the rejected *modi* are more numerous and far-reaching than those taken into consideration in the final alterations to the text. It is certain that this minority had submitted many other more important suggestions for change to the Holy Father, in fact nearly all their *modi* which had been rejected.

Paul VI wished to allow for the apprehensions of the minority which had been defeated when the vote on the *expensio modorum* was taken; at the same time, however, he wanted alterations to the wording to be restricted to those which seemed, in view of these apprehensions, necessary for any subsequent interpretation of the text. It was important to avoid anything which might give grounds for interpreting the text differently from the mind of the Council. The pope's intervention was accordingly made *ad majorem claritatem textus.*

But it is not true to say that the pope simply forced the alterations upon the Fathers of the Council, as some newspaper reports have suggested. As has already been said, the voting on the *expensio modorum* was not finished until Saturday, 14 November, 1964. The minority petition was submitted after this date to the pope, who then examined their arguments. Subsequently, on Wednesday, 18 November, Paul VI sent about forty suggestions for alteration to the Secretariat for Unity, and these were investigated and discussed by the directorate of the Secretariat in the only way possible in the short time available. The directorate of the Secretariat accepted just under half the alterations which had been sent to them—they considered that the intention, content and general tenor of the decree would not be affected by them. Everything had to be done in haste because the vote on the schema as a whole had to be taken on the following day, and at the same time the alterations had to be made known to the Fathers both orally and in writing. The solemn final sitting of the session was fixed for Saturday, 21 November, and for this reason it was no longer possible to convene a plenary session of the Secretariat for Unity.

In the 126th General Congregation on 19 November, 1964, the Secretary General of the Council announced that the final voting on the schema 'On Ecumenism' would take place the following day. He then read the nineteen corrections which were still to be inserted into the text, introducing them with the following declaration: 'Apart from the corrections already inserted, which had been accepted by the Council Fathers on the basis of the *modi*, the following have been added by the Secretariat for Unity in order to make the text clearer. In this way the Secretariat has accepted benevolent suggestions that had been authoritatively expressed.'

In the same session the Fathers received the texts of the corrections, with exact references by page and line to where they were to be inserted in the schema. In the afternoon they were able to study these corrections together with the schema and found that about 17 corrections concerned only matters of style and merely served to make the text clearer. The changes introduced into article 21 (The study of scripture) and article 22 (The sacramental life) carried more weight, but they did not constitute an essential change of content, especially if they are seen within the whole context of the articles. They evidently aimed at preventing misunderstandings on the part of Catholics and will be discussed later, when we treat the relevant sections in detail.

The voting on the schema 'On Ecumenism' which had

been printed on 19 November, 1964, took place on Friday, 20 November, 1964. The results were as follows: 2129 voted: 2054 in favour, 64 against, 11 invalid. The last solemn voting on the schema in the final session of the Council on Saturday, 21 November, 1964 had the following result: of the 2156 Fathers present, 2137 were in favour and 11 against the schema.

Pope Paul VI promulgated the decree 'On Ecumenism' in the words:

'The Fathers have resolved on each and every utterance in this decree. In virtue of the Apostolic power handed on to us from Christ, we join the venerable Fathers, in the Holy Spirit, in giving these utterances approval, decreeing them and enacting them. We order that the Synod's enactments be promulgated to the glory of God.'

He promulgated the dogmatic constitution *De Ecclesia*, and the decree 'On the Catholic Eastern Churches' with the same formula, in the same final session.

Part Two
Commentary on the Decree
with detailed explanation of the articles

1. Contents, Importance and Scope of the Decree

IN THE following pages we shall try to explain the individual articles of the decree 'On Ecumenism'. The term 'article' refers to the 24 items of the decree. When speaking of the discussion in the Council hall we always refer to the discussion of the first version of the schema during the second session of the Council, while references to the wishes, proposals, doubts, suggestions and observations of one or more Fathers always concern the written *modi* submitted in connection with the voting on the individual chapters of the second version of the schema during the third session. Similarly, the answers of the Secretariat for Unity always refer to its replies accepting or rejecting the *modi*, as given by the plenary meeting of the Secretariat. An alteration of the text on 19 November, 1964 refers to one of those emendations made by the Secretariat for Christian Unity which 'in this way . . . accepted benevolent suggestions that had been authoritatively expressed'. They were meant 'to make the text clearer': hence we shall try to explain the meaning and significance of these alterations which were inserted on the last day before the voting on the decree as a whole. Relevant suggestions are to be found in their place within the decree itself and in some of the *modi* submitted by the Fathers which had been worked on by the Secretariat for Unity. The examination confirmed what had been said by Cardinal Bea in his speech at Munich on 18 January: the alterations were in no way meant as an affront to our non-Catholic brothers; the changed text, properly understood, contains nothing that might hurt them. Misunderstandings have arisen through wrong translations from the Latin in various countries.

A proper understanding of the decree is hardly possible without considering all the *modi* examined by the Secretariat for Unity. The answers to the proposals and the reasons for their acceptance or rejection often throw much light on the meaning of a text, and the Council has agreed with the treatment of the *modi* by the Secretariat.

The terms 'church communities' or 'ecclesial communities' are both translations of the Latin *communitates ecclesiales*. '*Ecclesialis*' is a neologism which some Latin scholars prefer to *ecclesiasticus*, which is used with the same meaning in chapter three of the schema 'On the Church' (ecclesiastical communities).

In the translation of the decree the individual articles have been given those headings which had been provisionally inserted into the second version of the schema, but have been left out in the final Latin text.

The Fathers of the Council had been sorely tried during the final days of this session, yet in spite of this they showed remarkable equanimity and clarity of judgement when decisive matters were being put to the vote. This is especially true of the vote on the decree 'On Ecumenism'. When the nineteen alterations to the text were made known on Thursday, 19 November, the atmosphere in the Council was already extremely tense. In that same General Congregation Cardinal Tisserant had announced that the vote on the Declaration 'On Religious Liberty', would have to be postponed until the next session. This announcement caused much disappointment and consternation among many of the Fathers, and there was considerable speculation about the reasons for the postponement.

The completely revised text of the Declaration had been distributed on 17 November, and the Fathers were due to put it to the vote on 19 November. An appreciable minority complained to the Council authorities that they had not had sufficient time to study the document. Appealing to the *Ordo* of the Council they moved that the vote be postponed. Article 30, §2, of the *Ordo Concilii Vaticani II celebrandi* in fact lays down that the schemata of decrees and canons, as well as all texts to be submitted for approval, must be distributed to the Fathers in such a way that they have a suitable period of time to consider them, to reach a mature judgement and to decide which way they will vote. Seeing that the remaining texts had only just been distributed and were due to be discussed or put to the vote during the final days, this period of time was simply not available, quite apart from the fact that the submitted text could be considered as an entirely new one. Compared with the earlier draft the text of the Declaration was so lengthened and altered that, of the 556 lines of the new version, only 75 lines of the earlier one were included without any change. Under these circumstances and as a result of the minority petition, the presiding Council had decided that the voting would have to be postponed on the basis of article 30, §2, of the Council's *Ordo*. In their quite understandable desire to put the Declaration 'On Religious Liberty', to the vote, 441 Fathers of the majority turned to the Holy Father with a written petition to hasten a decision in their favour. Pope Paul VI referred the matter to the supervisory court of the Council, which is competent to pass judgement in such cases. The tribunal examined the petition and declared that the decision of the presidents of the Council was in full conformity with the Council's procedure. If the wish of the majority had been complied with, many of the Fathers would have been deprived of all opportunity of formulating and expressing their opinion as provided for in the *Ordo*. Thus Paul VI could have come to no other decision: the Council procedure had to be observed.

On calm reflection it was realized that the pope's decision was impartial and right, and made in accordance with his responsibility as a supreme arbiter who has to look beyond the present moment to the wider future implications. As *Le Monde* rightly said on 25 November, 1964: 'A pope is first and foremost an arbiter. Paul VI is so determined to fulfil this duty that he has not hesitated to risk being misunderstood either by a majority or by a minority.'

It is now generally recognized that the postponement of the voting was justified and that it enabled the text to be improved in the interim. In the commotion of the closing days, and lacking a detailed explanation of the reasons, many of the Fathers were extremely disturbed when they heard that the voting on the Declaration was to be put off until the fourth session. It was in this frame of mind that they learned also of the nineteen alterations to the text of the schema 'On Ecumenism'. As can be imagined, the atmosphere was distinctly unfavourable to any calm, rational appraisal of the changes. This accounts for the many bitter words of disillusionment, which were then greatly magnified in the press.

But the Fathers of the Council very quickly realized that the draft of the decree had not been altered in essentials and that if their voting produced a negative result it would jeopardize the preparatory work which the Secretariat for Unity and the Council had carried out for so many years. And so they voted in favour with an overwhelming majority. Their conviction that the decree was an exceedingly valuable document with vast implications for the future was a recognition of the true facts of the case which, even in the commotion of 'Black Thursday', could only momentarily be obscured. After a thorough examination of the alterations Congar wrote: 'After another careful reading of the three chapters "On Ecumenism" I can say in all truthfulness that their content and general purport remains unchanged. Any person reading them for the first time, and knowing nothing of the episode just recounted, would see nothing other than a candid, forthright declaration of the ecumenical attitude of a unanimous Catholic Church with the pope at its head. The text has certainly not been watered down. Three years ago none of us would have thought that it would meet with unanimous agreement in its present form. But we have no wish to influence anyone's mind in advance. We shall only say, like the voice which Augustine heard in the garden at Milan, *Tolle, lege—Take and read*. The text will speak for itself.'[1]

[1] Y. Congar, 'Introduction', op. cit. p. 169.

BISHOP PAUL

Servant of the servants of God
Together with the Fathers
of the sacred Council puts on
permanent record the

DECREE ON ECUMENISM

1. INTRODUCTION

1. Reunion among all Christians is a cause which the Second Vatican Ecumenical Council has set itself to promote as one of its principal aims. One single Church was founded by Christ the Lord, yet several Christian communions present themselves to mankind as the true heritage of Jesus Christ: they all claim to be the Lord's disciples but their views and the paths they tread are at variance, as if Christ himself has been divided up.[1] This division is in open contradiction to the will of Christ and the world finds it scandalous; it is damaging to the holy cause of preaching the gospel to every creature.

The text does not assert the restoration of unity to be one of the purposes of the Council, but the furthering of this unity, which may lead to its actual restoration.

The sentence saying that several Christian communions claim to be the true inheritance of Christ but tread different paths is a phenomenological description of an existing state. Hence, without commenting on it, the text merely expresses a fact that everyone can verify. This is clarified still further by

[1] Cf. 1 Cor. 1:13.

the insertion of 19 November, 1964. The text of the second version ran: 'The disciples of the Lord think and feel differently.' The final text supplements this by saying that all, indeed, claim to be disciples of the Lord, but that they are at variance in their views. This is a simple fact which everyone can verify and which is here briefly referred to as contrary to the foundation of the one Church by Jesus Christ.

The Lord of ages is wise and patient in the pursuit of the gracious plan that he has for us sinners. Though Christians are estranged from each other, in recent times he has begun to increase the spread among them of a heartfelt regret and longing for unity. This is a grace whose influence has been felt by men in great numbers all over the world. The grace of the Holy Spirit has encouraged the rise of a movement towards reunion among our separated brethren too, and this movement is growing daily. It has been given the name of the ecumenical movement. Its active members are those who call upon the God who is three, and who acknowledge Jesus Christ as Lord and Saviour. They do so not only as isolated individuals but in congregational groups in which they have heard the gospel and which they call, in each case, their Church, God's Church. Though they differ in the methods they adopt, almost all[1] their hearts are set on a single, visible Church of God, one which will be truly universal, on a mission to the whole world to bring glory to God by the conversion of the world to God and its consequent salvation.

The origin and growth of the ecumenical movement are attributed to the grace of the Holy Spirit, as had already been

---

[1] We have added to the C.T.S. translation here the words 'almost all' which are missing in the official English text. See below, p. 68; and the Latin text, 'Fere omnes . . . ad Ecclesiam Dei unam et visibilem adspirant. (Translator's note.)

done by the popes and also in the declaration of the Holy
Office of 20 December, 1949.

According to the second version of the schema the
ecumenical movement had originated in the desire to achieve
(*assequendam*) the unity of all Christians. It was suggested in
one of the *modi* that this unity of Christians had already
existed before the eleventh century. In order to comply with
this wish *assequendam* was replaced by *restaurandam* (restore).
This alteration, however, was not meant to imply that no
divisions had existed even before the eleventh century.
Furthermore, the 'restoration' of unity does not envisage the
return to an earlier historical state. The decree as a whole as
well as the constitution *De Ecclesia* constantly mentions the
road of salvation, history and the living growth of the
pilgrim Church.

*The sacred Synod is gladdened by these considerations. Now
that it has made its statement of the teaching on the Church, it is
activated by a longing for the reunion of all Christ's disciples. Its
present wish is to put before all Catholics the aids, the ways and
the means to enable them to correspond with this divine call, this
grace.*

This paragraph contains two statements which are
important for the explanation of the decree.

1. The decree presupposes the teaching of the dogmatic
constitution *De Ecclesia*, which is necessary for the proper
understanding of its ecclesiological statements. On the other
hand the decree is likewise important for the explanation of
the constitution, as Pope Paul VI has explicitly stated in his
final allocution in the Council hall on 21 November, 1964:
'We hope that our still separated brothers in Christ will

consider the same teaching on the Church with a right and benevolent intention. How greatly we desire that this doctrine, completed by the explanations contained in the schema "On Ecumenism" also approved by the Council, might awaken their spirit like a leaven of love, so that they may consider their intentions in such a way as to approach our community more and more closely and finally, please God, may be in it the same as we.'

2. The decree 'On Ecumenism' is addressed to Catholics and has a pastoral purpose. It wants to show Catholic Christians how they can share in the world-embracing ecumenical movement. In his Rome press conference of 11 November, 1964, Dr. Lukas Vischer rightly said: 'In the new text the introduction ... points explicitly to the existence of the ecumenical movement and makes it clear that it is not intended to be a Magna Carta for the whole ecumenical movement but only to make clear the attitude of the Roman Catholic Church to this movement. This change seems promising to me. If this knowledge is put into practice, co-operation among the Churches will be considerably easier.' This is followed by a clear hint at the basic formula of the World Council of Churches: 'The World Council of Churches is a community of Churches who confess the Lord Jesus Christ as God and Saviour according to the scriptures and therefore endeavour to accomplish what they are called to do, to the glory of God, the Father, the Son and the Holy Spirit.'

The statement of the second version, that all aspire to the one visible Church, has been modified in the final text of 19 November, 1964, by an 'almost', which is more in accordance with the facts.

The New Delhi report of the section on unity clearly emphasizes the desire for visible unity: 'We believe that the unity which is both God's will and his gift to his Church is being made visible as all in each place who are baptized into Jesus Christ and confess him as Lord and Saviour are brought by the Holy Spirit into one fully committed fellowship, holding the one apostolic faith, preaching the one gospel, breaking the one bread, joining in common prayer, and having a corporate life reaching out in witness and service to all and who at the same time are united with the whole Christian fellowship in all places and all ages in such a wise that ministry and members are accepted by all and that all can act and speak together as occasion requires for the tasks to which God calls his people.'[1]

[1] *The New Delhi Report*, SCM Press 1962, p. 116.

2. Chapter One: Catholic Principles of Ecumenism

INSTEAD of the heading of the first version 'On the Principles of Catholic Ecumenism' that of the second version, 'On the Catholic Principles of Ecumenism' has been retained. As has been said before, this change was very important. The decree recognizes the existence of a world-wide ecumenical movement and invites Catholics to participate in it according to their own Catholic principles. Together with many other Fathers, Archbishop Casimiro Morcillo of Saragossa had demanded the change of title during the second session, giving the following reason: 'It accords better with the special character of the Council as far as possible to agree to and confirm whatever is profitable for our time. But to propagate a Catholic ecumenism would mean directly to contradict the "ecumenical movement", to overlook the not yet sufficiently explored possibilities of ecumenism and to duplicate the ecumenical effort instead of strengthening it by harmonious co-operation.'

Yves Congar has pointed out that the change of title implies a very important statement, which is particularly topical in the new ecumenical situation produced by the Council. It has been expressed in the allocutions of Paul VI on the unity of Christians and in his meeting with the Patriarch Athenagoras.

THE UNITY AND UNIQUENESS OF THE CHURCH

2. What has revealed the love of God, where we are concerned, is the mission on which the only-begotten Son of God was sent into the world by the Father. He was to be made man, to ransom the whole human race, give it fresh birth, bring it together into one.[1] Before he made the offering of himself—he, the unspotted victim, the cross his altar—the Son of God prayed to the Father on behalf of believers with these words: 'That they may all be one; that they too may be one in us, as thou, Father, art in me, and I in thee; so that the world may come to believe that it is thou who hast sent me' (John 17:21). He also founded the eucharist in his Church, the wonderful sacrament which indicates and brings about the Church's unity. He gave his disciples the new commandment of love for each other[2] and promised them the Holy Spirit who would befriend them,[3] the Lord and giver of life who would stay with them for ever.

The second version said of the high-priestly prayer of Jesus: he prayed to the Father for the faithful. One Father pointed out that, according to the Greek original of John 17:20, it should be 'believers' rather than 'faithful'. The small alteration was accepted and appears in the final text.

The eucharist as the sign and efficient cause of the Church's unity is emphasized in the same way as in the constitutions 'On the Liturgy' and 'On the Church'. According to the principle 'the sacraments effect what they signify' the unity of the Church is signified and effected by the eucharist, as was implied by the eucharistic prayers of the *Didache* as early as the first half of the second century. In the West this

---

[1] 1 John 4:9; Col. 1:18-20; John 11:52.
[2] Cf. John 13:34.   [3] Cf. John 16:7.

doctrine was developed especially by St Augustine; St Thomas Aquinas incorporated it in the eucharistic teaching of his *Summa Theologica*. The same doctrine has been expanded in the East, especially by Cyril of Jerusalem, Cyril of Alexandria and Chrysostom. At the end of the paragraph the Holy Spirit is called Lord and giver of life in obvious dependence on the Creed.

Once he had been lifted up on the cross and entered his glory, the Lord Jesus poured out the Spirit that he had promised. The Spirit is the agent through whom he has uttered his call to the people of the New Covenant, the Church, and brought it together in the unity of faith, hope and charity. This is the teaching of the apostle: 'You are one body, with a single spirit; each of you when he was called, called in the same hope; with the same Lord, the same faith, the same baptism' (Eph. 4:4-5). Elsewhere he explains: 'All you who have been baptized in Christ's name have put on the person of Christ ... you are all one person in Jesus Christ' (Gal. 3:27-8). The Holy Spirit makes his dwelling in believers; he impregnates and controls the whole Church. He is responsible for the fellowship of the faithful that is so remarkable; he gives them a deep attachment to each other in Christ. He is thus the principle of the Church's unity. The different kinds of gifts and of service are his work.[1] He enriches the Church with a variety of gifts 'to order the lives of the faithful, minister to their needs, build up the frame of Christ's body' (Eph. 4:12).

In this section several scriptural passages of the first version were left out or replaced by others in the second version: e.g. Rom. 6:4 by Gal. 3:27f. Eph. 4:16, which had been quoted in connection with the ministry of the Church, was omitted. Eph. 2:20 ('upon the foundation of the apostles and

[1] Cf. 1 Cor. 12: 4-11.

prophets') has also been left out, because some exegetes refer these words not to the apostles of the New and the prophets of the Old Covenant, but to the offices and charisms of the primitive Church. In quotation of Gal. 3:28 the neuter *unum* (one) of the Vulgate was replaced by the masculine *unus*, in accordance with the Greek original. Four Fathers had wanted this, and the passage has also been quoted in this form in article 32 of the constitution 'On the Church'.

Here the pneumatological aspect of the Church and its unity is particularly emphasized. The Eastern Churches have always considered this decisive and have closely connected it with the eucharist. Pius XII says in his encyclical *Mystici Corporis*: 'This Spirit of Christ is the invisible principle to which we must also attribute the union of all the parts of the Body with one another and with their exalted Head, dwelling as he does whole in the Head, whole in the Body, and whole in each of its members . . . the divine Spirit, who, in the words of the Angelic Doctor, "numerically one and the same, fills and unifies the whole Church".'[1]

At the beginning of this paragraph the second version had 'The Lord Jesus poured out the Spirit that he had promised, by whom (*quo*). . .'. One Council Father proposed rather 'through whom' (*per quem*), because the Holy Spirit was personally effective in calling and uniting Christians. This was done in the final text.

The text stating that the Holy Spirit dwells in believers (*credentes*) takes this word as meaning those who have a faith vivified by love. Eph. 3:17 says that Christ dwells in their hearts by faith; this implies also the indwelling of the Holy Spirit.

[1] Eng. trans. C.T.S., 1944, n. 55 and 60.

The expression 'different kinds of gifts and of service' is suggested by 1 Cor. 12:4 'There are varieties of gifts', hence the singular of the second version was replaced by the plural.

To secure a world-wide stability for his Church until the consummation of the world, Christ entrusted the office of teaching, government and sanctification to the college made up of the Twelve. Among them he selected Peter: when Peter had made his profession of faith, he decided to build his Church upon him; he promised him the keys of the kingdom of heaven.[2] When Peter had made his profession of love, he commissioned him to give all the sheep support in their belief[3] and to tend them in perfect unity.[4] Jesus Christ was to remain the chief corner-stone for ever[5] and the pastor of our souls.[6]

The mention of the college of apostles corresponds to the teaching of the constitution 'On the Church' on the collegiality of the apostles and their successors. Nothing is said about the exact date at which Jesus gave the apostles their authority. The sentences following, on the primacy of Peter, also correspond to the constitution 'On the Church'. For brevity's sake the classical texts on the primacy are not cited verbatim; they are presupposed in the context and commented on. The text follows the historical sequence: after Peter's election he is promised and finally given the primacy. The historical perfect is used to describe how Peter was raised to the highest pastoral office. The words 'decided to build' point to the manifestation of the will of the Lord in the promise of the primacy. The classical text Luke 22: 32 is

[1] Cf. Mt. 28:18-20; cp. John 20:21-23.
[2] Cf. Mt. 16:19, cp. Mt. 18:18.   [3] Cf. Luke 22:32.
[4] Cf. John 21:15-17.   [5] Cf. Eph. 2:20.
[6] Cf. 1 Peter 2:25; Vatican Council I, Sess. IV (1870), Constitution *Pastor aeternus*: Coll. Lac. 7, 482 a.

suggested by the term 'support' but not actually quoted. The grammatical form (*confirmandas*) indicates that Jesus spoke these words before conferring the pastoral office. Incidentally, exegetes are not agreed whether the term 'brothers' in this passages refers only to the apostles or to all the faithful. According to the original text of the schema the pastoral office was conferred on Peter 'after the profession of greater love'. Six Council Fathers pointed out that Peter had replied to the question 'Do you love me more than these' only 'You know that I love you' (John 21:15-17). Hence the final text reads simply: 'When Peter had made his profession of love.' On 14 January, 1965, Paul VI said in an address to the patricians and noblemen of the city of Rome: 'We live in the kingdom of love which was founded by Jesus Christ, the "shepherd of shepherds", as St Augustine called him, and which, as the gospel reports, derived in the heart of Peter from that love which the apostle had for the Master, and which the Master directed from himself towards the flock, that is to mankind: he made the lover the shepherd, as St Augustine says in the same passage.[1] Jesus has formed the lover into the shepherd. We know the fullness of meaning the lovely and tragic image of the shepherd is given in the language of the gospel: the meaning of a wholly undeserved, selfless and watchful love that is perfectly surrendered, generous and heroic.'[2]

The paragraph concludes with the statement that Christ himself remains the corner-stone and the shepherd of our souls for all eternity. The primacy of Peter and his successors accords with this, as Pope Paul VI has also emphasized, for

[1] *Sermo* 138, 5; Migne, *Patrologia Latina* 38, 765.
[2] *Osservatore Romano* of 15 January 1965, p. 1.

example in his opening addresses for the second and third sessions of the Council.

The work of the apostles and their successors—that is to say, the bishops with Peter's successor as their head—is to preach the gospel with loyalty, to administer the sacraments, and to govern with love. These are the means by which Jesus Christ wants the Holy Spirit to work the growth of his people; the means too whereby he brings their fellowship to complete unity in the acknowledgement of a single faith, the celebration of divine worship in common and the harmony of brothers in the household of God.

The second version of the schema did not contain the words 'that is to say the bishops with Peter's successor as their head'. Hence several Fathers were of the opinion that the inner elements of the unity of the Church had, rightly indeed, been stressed in this whole article, but for the sake of balance the external elements, and especially the primacy, ought also to be mentioned. Hence the addition in the final text. This has now a deliberately introduced parallelism between the preaching of the gospel, the administration of the sacraments and the guidance in love on the one hand, and the one creed, the common liturgical celebration and the brotherly concord on the other.

The mention of the 'household of God' had been desired especially by the African Fathers. The final text has inserted this because in the New Testament all the faithful are called a family of God and also because the expression is frequently found in the liturgy.

The expression 'celebration in common' is in accordance with the terminology of the constitution 'On the Liturgy' and is in general use today.

The Church, then, is God's only flock; it is, as it were, a standard set up among the nations;[1] *it is the minister of the gospel of peace to the whole human race*[2] *as, full of hope, it makes its pilgrimage towards the homeland on high which is its goal.*[3]

The expression 'a standard set up among the nations' emphasizes the visibility and knowability of the Church, as had already been done by the First Vatican Council in chapter three of the constitution 'On the Catholic Faith'.

The theme of the pilgrim Church, borne up by eschatological hope, is treated extensively in the constitution 'On the Church'. The term *meta*, goal, is found in scripture and is particularly well suited to the image of the pilgrim Church.

This is the sacred mystery of the Church's unity. The unity is established in Christ and through Christ, while the variety of gifts is the work of the Holy Spirit. The mystery has its supreme model and its starting-point in the unity of Persons in the Trinity, the unity of the one God, Father and Son in the Holy Spirit.

The Trinity is worshipped as the exemplar and principle of the unity of the Church, which is a mystery in Christ and the Holy Spirit. The formula 'the unity of the one God, Father and Son in the Holy Spirit' is used by the Fathers and theologians of the Church to signify the Holy Spirit as the bond of love between Father and Son.

The report of the section on unity of the World Council of Churches at New Delhi begins with the words: 'The love of the Father and the Son in the unity of the Holy Spirit is the source and goal of the unity which the Triune God wills for all men and creation. We believe that we share in this unity in the Church of Jesus Christ ... The Lord who is bringing all things into full unity at the last is he who con-

---

[1] Cf. Is. 11:10-12.
[2] Cf. Eph. 2:17 f, together with Mark 16:5.   [3] Cf. 1 Peter 1:3-9.

strains us to seek the unity which he wills for his Church on earth here and now.'[1]

Summary

In accordance with the constitution 'On the Church', article two of the decree treated of the unity and uniqueness of the Church, of the primacy of the pope and the powers of the apostolic college of bishops. Dr Lukas Vischer said in his press conference in Rome on 11 November, 1964: 'The decree "On Ecumenism" makes clear the ecclesiological terms on which the Roman Catholic Church intends to join in the ecumenical conversations. The uniqueness and unity of the Roman Catholic Church are unmistakably emphasized, and it is clear that these statements and the consequences necessarily following from them will always provoke the opposition of the non-Roman Churches, be they orthodox or Protestant . . . This statement is not meant as a criticism. Nobody could expect essential changes in this matter. The texts have confirmed this. In some respects we may even be grateful that this has been made so clear. For the fact that the differences have not been glossed over will help us to recognize the real question which confronts us today.'

Dr Vischer says elsewhere: 'The non-Roman Churches do not deny that the Roman Catholic Church must declare itself to be the one and only Church. But if a constant dialogue between the separated Churches is to develop, a way must be found which does not force the non-Roman Churches to accept the Roman Catholic conception of unity and union even during the period of the dialogue'.[2]

[1] *The New Delhi Report*, p. 116.
[2] L. Vischer, 'L'Église communauté de l'Esprit', in *Lumière et Vie* 67, p. 39.

Certainly, no Catholic theologian means to bring such pressure to bear. For Catholics the questions of the uniqueness and primacy of the Church involve faithfulness to the mystery of Christ, to the Word of God, and to the apostolicity and eschatological character of the Church. We understand very well that our Protestant brethren, from their different point of view, think that we are wrong about these questions. But it pertains to the ecumenical attitude that they should be prepared to listen to our questions and to answer our arguments from scripture and the apostolic tradition. For these questions bind us in conscience. It is evident that the ecclesiological principles governing our ecumenical dialogue raise grave problems for the non-Catholics. But is the reverse not equally true? The ecclesiological principles of Protestantism are just as difficult for the Catholic side of the dialogue. It is essential to ecumenism that we should listen to each other and talk to one another firmly determined to obey the Word of God. Oscar Cullman has pointed out these conditions for the ecumenical dialogue in an article published by *Le Monde* on 4/5 November, 1964. The decree 'On Ecumenism' expressed a new relationship of mutual trust in which such a dialogue can become ever more effective.

THE RELATION OF THE SEPARATED BRETHREN TO THE CATHOLIC CHURCH

3. From the very beginning, divisions have appeared in this Church which is one and unique;[1] *the apostle uttered a strongly worded condemnation of them.*[2] *Succeeding ages have seen the birth*

[1] Cf. 1 Cor. 11:18-19; Gal. 1:6-9; 1 John 2:18-19.
[2] Cf. 1 Cor. 1:11 ff.; 11:22.

of greater quarrels, and communities of considerable size have broken away from full fellowship in the Catholic Church. The fault has sometimes been on both sides; there can be no question of charging the men who have been born and steeped in belief in Christ in these communities with the sin of separation. The Catholic Church surrounds them with the respect and love one shows to brothers. Men who believe in Christ and who have duly received baptism are established in a fellowship with the Catholic Church, even if the fellowship be incomplete. There are various real points of disagreement between them and the Catholic Church on matters of doctrine and discipline and on the question of the Church's structural organization. These disagreements provide many impediments, and, in some cases, serious obstacles in the way of full fellowship with the Church. It is the aim of the ecumenical movement to surmount these obstructions. Despite the disagreements, men whose faith has brought them acceptance with God in baptism are incorporated in Christ.[1] It is right they should be distinguished with the name of Christian and they deserve to be recognized by the children of the Catholic Church as their brothers in the Lord.[2]

In this description, as in the whole of the first chapter of the decree, no difference is made between orthodox and reformed Christians in their relation to the Catholic Church. This follows only in the third chapter.

The divisions that were already present in the early Church did not only violate charity but, like those which occurred later, also involved truths of faith and originated in a different interpretation of the apostolic message. We need

---

[1] Cf. Council of Florence, Sess. VIII (1439), Decree *Exultate Deo:* Mansi 31, 1055 A.

[2] Cf. St Augustine, *In Ps.* 32, *Enarr.* II, 29:PL 36, 299.

only recall the heresies mentioned and opposed in the pastoral epistles, in Ignatius of Antioch, St Irenaeus and Tertullian. But the decree does not mean to imply that there never has been a united Church and that Christendom has been divided from the beginning. The unity of the Church is given by God in Christ and through the Holy Spirit; it is not first to be produced by the faithful and it is not destroyed by divisions.

The decree says that in the following centuries larger communities became separated from the full communion of the Catholic Church. The communion of the Church is not to be understood only juridically; it also includes sacramental and spiritual elements, which are not equally present in all the communities separated from the Catholic Church. The decree distinguishes the perfect communion of all individual Catholic churches from the non-perfect communion by which the separated churches and ecclesial communities are still joined to the Catholic Church.

The separations are sometimes due to the fault of men on either side. It is a historical truth that Catholic Christians, the hierarchy as well as the faithful, had their share of the guilt. In his *relatio* on Part One of the third chapter of 7 October, 1964, Archbishop Maximos Hermaniuk had mentioned the partial responsibility of Cardinal Humbert for the beginning of the schism in 1054. The partial responsibility of Catholics for the divisions of the sixteenth century was mentioned by Aegidius of Viterbo at the Fifth Lateran Council, by Pope Hadrian VI through his Nuncio Chieregati at the Diet of Nuremberg in 1522-3, by Cardinal Pole and by many other Fathers of the Council of Trent. The decree does not go into historical details but says only that in some cases human guilt was present on both sides. The possibility is left open that the origin of a division may also in some cases be attributable to one side only. It is noteworthy, too, that the decree does not mention the actual act of separation, but the causes which prepared and finally effected it. A decisive difference is made between those Christians who were alive at the time and co-operated in the division and those who were later born into these separated communities and who cannot be held responsible for the separation which took place before their time. A number of Fathers had asked for the words 'provided they are in good faith and sincerely seek the true Church' to be added. The decree has not complied with this wish because we presuppose that our separated brethren are in good faith. The principles of Christian conduct demand that we should presuppose good faith in others as long as the opposite has not clearly been proved. Without this principle no ecumenical activity is possible.

The decree then places side by side three statements in which both the possibilities and the difficulties of ecumenism are clearly expressed.

1. All those who believe in Christ and have been validly baptized are in real, though not in perfect, communion with the Catholic Church.

2. The separation has deep causes, and these the ecumenical movement wants to overcome. The second version of the schema mentioned grounds that divide Catholic Christians and those separated from them. Seven Fathers observed here that doctrinal differences concern not only the faithful but the whole Church, especially as they are for a large part directly ecclesiological. Hence in the final text the words 'the faithful of the Catholic Church' were replaced

by 'the Catholic Church'. The expression 'on matters of doctrine and discipline' suggests that there may also be disciplinary reasons for the separation which are not so grave as doctrinal differences.

3. Those justified by faith through baptism are incorporated in Christ and rightly bear the name Christian. The text avoids the expression 'they are incorporated in the mystical Body of Christ' so as not to raise again the question of the Church membership of non-Catholics which had been so violently discussed after the encyclical *Mystici Corporis*. There is no doubt that according to St Paul those justified by faith through baptism are incorporated in Christ. Since the apostle makes more frequent use of the formula *ex fide*, the decree has this instead of the *per fidem* of the second version.

Moreover a number of the important elements or gifts from which the Church derives its structure and life are capable of an existence beyond the confines of the visible Catholic Church. The majority of them in fact do so exist: the written Word of God, the life of grace, faith, hope and charity, and other inward gifts and visible elements from the Holy Spirit. They all have their origin and their conclusion in Christ: they belong by right to Christ's Church.

'Of the important elements or gifts from which the Church derives its structure and life' is not meant to indicate that the Church is built up through a simple addition of all ecclesial elements. Rather do all these elements form an organic unity in the only Church of Christ, as is clear from the present decree as well as from the constitution *De Ecclesia*.

The plenitude of catholicity may on no account be understood in a merely quantitative sense. The fullness of truth and grace means more than a numerical completeness of the deposit of faith and the means of salvation. The fullness indicates a transition to the qualitative order; it means perfection and an integral wholeness that admit of neither more nor less. Only the 'fullness' guarantees the coherence of the whole and the importance of its individual parts. For this reason the decree does not understand the relation of Protestantism to Catholicism simply in a quantitative way.

The text expresses a complex reality. On the one hand the separated churches and ecclesial communities are outside the confines of the Catholic Church, on the other the separated brethren and their communities are already in incomplete communion with the Catholic Church, because they have preserved some ecclesial elements that belong by right to the one Church of Christ. The words 'by right' belong to the corrections inserted on 19 November, 1964 and had somehow already been contained in 'belong'.

It was suggested in one of the *modi* that the clause 'all these ... belong' ought to be replaced by a quotation from St Augustine: 'All these are gifts with which Christ enriches his unique Spouse.' This was acknowledged to be both apposite and beautiful; it was not, however, included so as to avoid unnecessary alterations.

The efficacy of the ecclesial elements comes to the separated churches from Christ through the Holy Spirit. Through these elements the separated churches share already in the good of unity, though not in complete unity. The text of the decree states what is lacking.

Only some examples are given in the enumeration of the ecclesial elements in the separated churches and ecclesial communities; completeness is not intended. Since orthodox as well as reformed communities are mentioned in this section, only some generally preserved ecclesial elements are mentioned; they are described more exactly in the two parts of chapter three.

Many too of the sacred actions of the Christian religion are performed among our separated brethren. There is no doubt that they are capable of giving real birth to the life of grace, in ways which differ according to the different nature of the individual church or community, and it must be granted that they are capable of giving admission to the community of salvation.

The phrase 'the sacred actions of the Christian religion are performed' points to saving actions accomplished by the communities. The formula is very general, because it must be applicable to reformed as well as to orthodox Christians, since these are treated separately only in chapter three. The passage concerns sacraments or actions that have effects similar to those of the sacraments. They can mediate the life of grace, good faith being always presupposed.

True, these saving actions do not produce full communion with the Catholic Church, but they are in themselves apt to open up the entrance to the full communion of salvation.

Even though we believe that these churches[1] or communities are defective, they are certainly not without significance and importance in the mystery of salvation. Christ's Spirit has not refused to employ them as means of salvation. Their strength derives from the very fullness of grace and truth entrusted to the Catholic Church.

The term 'churches or communities' is used by the

---

[1] Cf. Fourth Lateran Council (1215), Constitutio IV: Mansi 22, 990. Second Council of Lyons (1274), Profession of Faith of Michael Paleologus: Mansi 24, 71 E; Council of Florence Session VI (1439), definition Laetentur cadi: Mansi 31, 1026 E.

Council without its being determined which of the separated Western communities should be called churches in the theological sense. God uses the churches and ecclesial communities for giving saving graces to their Christian members. He does not use them insofar as they are separated, but insofar as they have preserved the ecclesial elements mentioned before. Where the means of salvation that are the common actions of the separated communions are validly administered, the Holy Spirit uses these communities and communions as means for salvation. Their saving efficacy derives from that fullness of grace and truth (John 1:14) which Christ has entrusted to the Catholic Church.

The second version had stated that this fullness of grace had been entrusted to the Church; on 19 November, 1964 the word Catholic was added to Church. This addition did not change the meaning, for a few lines later it is expressly stated that the fullness of all the means of salvation can be had only through the Catholic Church.

All the same, our separated brethren do not have the benefit, as individuals or in their communities and churches, of the unity which Jesus Christ has wanted to bestow on all those to whom he has given rebirth into a single body and into the new life, with the gift of a life in common; this is the unity proclaimed by the sacred scriptures and by the venerable tradition of the Church. Only through the Catholic Church of Christ, the universal aid to salvation, can the means of salvation be reached in all their fullness. It is our belief that Christ entrusted all the benefits of the New Covenant to the apostolic college over which Peter presides. His purpose was the establishment in the world of a single body of Christ; all those who already belong in some way to God's people ought to have full incorporation in it. This people may remain liable to sin in its members for the duration of its pilgrimage on earth, but it has growth in Christ and gentle guidance from God, who is pursuing his secret designs, until it shall have the joy of arriving at the full completion of eternal glory in the heavenly Jerusalem.

In accordance with the desire of many Fathers the second version of the schema here stressed clearly that the Church is necessary for salvation, that it is faithful in preaching the true doctrine and that Christ himself has made it one. It also explains the visibility of the Church and the importance of the hierarchy. Christ has entrusted all saving graces directly to the apostles and through them to the Church. Hence the Church is by no means identified with the college of apostles, for it is clear from the context that all the riches of salvation the New Covenant possesses are entrusted to the whole Church through the apostles. The schema carefully refrains from identifying the Church with the hierarchy. The phrase 'it is our belief that Christ entrusted' refers to strictly theological faith.

The present tense in 'over which Peter presides' includes also his successors. True, Peter is distinguished from the college of apostles, but it is equally clear that he belongs to it. These statements are in accordance with the third chapter of the constitution *De Ecclesia*.

The paragraph finally mentions the historical aspect of the pilgrim Church, whose members are always threatened by weakness, temptation and sin. On 17 October, 1963, the spokesman of the observer delegates, Professor Skydsgaard, had said at a reception of Pope Paul VI: 'I may be permitted here to point out something that seems very important to me: I refer to the role of a biblical theology that concentrates on the study of salvation history in the Old and New Testaments. The more we progress in understanding the mysterious and paradoxical history of the people of God the more we begin really to understand the Church of Jesus Christ both in its mystery and in its historical existence and its unity.'

To this wish of Professor Skydsgaard that the Council should take an increasing interest in such concrete and historical theology Pope Paul replied: 'We on our part gladly assent to the development you desire of a "concrete and historical" theology which concentrates on salvation history. It seems to us that this suggestion deserves to be thoroughly examined. The Catholic Church has institutions which are in no way prevented from specializing more in such research, or it may even create a new institute if circumstances should require it.'

In an address to the observer delegates on 29 September, 1964, the Pope mentioned again 'the foundation of an institute for salvation history, which should in some way be accomplished by a common effort'.

In the constitution *De Ecclesia* as well as in the decree 'On Ecumenism' salvation history is more strongly emphasized than in the first drafts. The second version had said of the people of God: 'This people may remain liable to sin . . . but it has constant growth in Christ.' The final text has two alterations:

1. The words 'in its members' are inserted. This addition was made on 19 November, 1964; it is meant to make clear that in its institutions established by Christ, for example in the sacraments, the Church is not liable to sin, but it is so liable in its earthly members who, being human, 'must look

forward with fear to the battle that is still to be fought with the flesh, the world and the devil'.[1]

2. Some Fathers had objections to the word 'constant'. They asked whether it could really be said that the Church was constantly growing. Had there not been periods in Church history during which the number of confessors and saints had not increased? Are there not in many members of the pilgrim Church times of stagnation and decay? This *modus* was accepted and the word 'constant' was dropped. The Secretariat for Unity was well aware of the fact that this term could be understood of the general growth of the Church from the times of the apostles to the present. Thus the First Vatican Council had also spoken of the marvellous expansion of the Church and its inexhaustible fruitfulness.[2]

ECUMENISM

4. Nowadays, the grace of the Holy Spirit is encouraging, in many parts of the world, a great number of efforts by way of prayer, word and work to reach the full completion of unity, which is the desire of Jesus Christ. This sacred Synod therefore calls upon all the Catholic faithful to recognize the signs of the times and to play an informed part in the work of ecumenism.

By 'ecumenical movement' is meant all the activities and attempts which are initiated and co-ordinated for the purpose of encouraging the unity of Christians; they vary with the needs of the Church and the moments of opportunity. Such are, in the first place, all the efforts made to do away with terms, decisions and actions when they do not fairly and truly correspond to the position

[1] Council of Trent, 6th Session, 13th chapter; Denzinger 806.

[2] Third Session, chapter 3; Denzinger 1794.

of the separated brethren and so make for greater difficulty in our mutual dealings. Secondly there is the initiation of 'dialogue' between competent experts at meetings of the Christians of different churches and communities, which are arranged with a religious motive in view. This dialogue involves on the part of each participant an explanation at a deeper level of the doctrine of his communion and a clear presentation of its characteristics. It enables everyone to acquire a truer understanding and a fairer estimate of the doctrine and life of the other's communion. Another good effect is the fuller collaboration that the communions achieve in the case of duties, which are demanded by every Christian conscience, for the common good, as well as their agreement in prayer at meetings which they hold, where it is allowed. Finally they all submit to scrutiny their loyalty to the will of Christ with regard to the Church and, where necessary, make a vigorous start on the work of renewal and reform.

The second version of the schema corresponded to the wishes of many Fathers for a complete and clearer explanation of ecumenism. As has been said before, a scholastic definition according to genus and specific difference was impossible. Ecumenism is a movement started by the breathing of the Holy Spirit whose future progress cannot be mapped out, though we know that the Spirit wishes to lead it to the unity of all Christians in the one Church of Jesus Christ.

The text gives a description from which the essential characteristics of ecumenism can easily be recognized. While in the first version the descriptive elements had been scattered somewhat disorderly throughout article four, these are now put in better order and more are added. The article first describes what is meant by ecumenism and then states

the principles which make it possible for Catholics to participate in the ecumenical movement.

The second version had started with the words 'Today,
under the breathing of the Holy Spirit' (*Cum hodie . . . Spiritu
Sancto afflante*). The *modi* of seven Fathers suggested that
since Pius XII's encyclical *Divino afflante Spiritu* of 30
September, 1943 these words were normally referred to the
inspiration of scripture. Hence they suggested the insertion
of the word grace, which would also correspond to the
terminology of the Instruction of the Holy Office of 20
December, 1949. The Secretariat for Unity, though not
insensitive to the proposal, rejected the change because it
seemed unnecessary. It was only made on 19 November,
1964, together with the other eighteen changes inserted into
the text on this date.

Where the decree mentions all ecclesial communities and
churches including the Catholic Church it uses the term
communions, which had already been employed by St
Augustine for designating both Catholic and Donatist
Churches. The use of this term had been recommended some
time ago by Yves Congar.

The term *fratres separati* of the first version has everywhere
been replaced by *fratres seiuncti*. This small change is important, because to the modern mind *separati* might have a
negative nuance whereas *seiuncti* merely states the fact of the
separation.

In the last line renewal and reform are placed side by
side.

Two Fathers considered this to be superfluous and proposed to leave out the word reform (*reformatio*). This *modus*
was not accepted, because renewal and reform are not the

same thing and because earlier Councils, too, frequently used the term reform.[1]

All this activity contributes to the advance of justice and truth, harmony and collaboration, brotherly spirit and unity, when its performance by the faithful of the Catholic Church is marked by patience and prudence and watched over by the bishops. This is the road which leads over the obstacles to complete communion, to the gathering of all Christians at a single celebration of the eucharist in the unity of the one and only Church. This unity was bestowed by Christ on his Church at the beginning, we believe that it is still in existence in the Catholic Church and cannot be lost; we hope it will continue to increase daily until the consummation of the world.

One Father had suggested that this whole section should be inserted in Chapter Two, because it dealt rather with the practice of ecumenism. But the Secretariat for Unity rightly thought that these and the following paragraphs presented the Catholic principles of ecumenism more concretely and that one could not make a mathematical division between the exposition of the principles and the explanation of their practical application.

While in article two of this chapter the eucharist had been stated to be the symbol and efficacious basis of the unity of the Church, in the present passage the common celebration of the eucharist is regarded as the strongest symbolic expression of the desired unity when this will have been achieved. In the Catholic Church Christ has established a unity that cannot be lost; but it is capable of growing until the end of the ages. The term 'we believe' is here understood

[1] Cf. the collection in the Index of *Conciliorum Oecumenicorum Decreta*, Freiburg i. Br. 1962, p. 39*, s.v. *reformatio ecclesiae*.

in the strictly theological sense of supernatural faith.

There is clearly an essential distinction between the work of preparing and reconciling individuals who desire full communion with the Catholic Church and the ecumenical undertaking. There is no conflict between them, for they are both the development of the admirable plan of God.

The official *relatio* on the second version of the schema says: 'It would be a quite wrong view of ecumenism if it were to be regarded as a new tactics for achieving conversions more easily. True, the apostolate of reconciling individuals should also be recognized as a work of the Holy Spirit and is in no way opposed to the work of ecumenism. But that apostolate differs essentially from the ecumenical movement, which has a different object and is of a different nature. All this is stated in a special section that has been inserted in the amended text.'

Consequently the second version of the schema had the following text: 'Hence it is clear that there is no opposition between this ecumenical action and the apostolate of reconciliation of those individuals who want to join the Catholic Church, though they are different in nature, because both are works inspired by the Holy Spirit.'

Not all the Fathers agreed with this new paragraph. One *modus* proposed the following text: 'From what has been said so far it is clear that there is an essential difference between ecumenical activity and the work of individual reconciliation. For while this work concerns those who, following their conscience, want to enter the Catholic Church and must be suitably prepared for this, ecumenical activity intends the union of the churches and communities as such, and this union cannot be hoped from God except through the renewal of all. But as both works are inspired by the Holy Spirit there is no opposition between them, and the difficulties can be overcome if every semblance of proselytism is avoided and mutual trust between the churches and communities is encouraged.'

This proposal contained important suggestions, but it would have had to be further clarified, especially with regard to proselytism. Another *modus* proposed the text that now appears in the decree, the final sentence of which originally ran: 'as both proceed from the action of the Holy Spirit.'

The *modus* gave the following reasons:

(*a*) the term 'apostolate' is better suited to the evangelization of non-Christians. If it is used in connexion with conversions, non-Catholic Christians suspect 'proselytism'.[1]

(*b*) The second version of the decree mentions first ecumenism and then the apostolate of conversions. The reversed order should be used so as to avoid every semblance of conversions being the true end of ecumenism.

(*c*) The expression 'to join the Catholic Church' was less suitable for describing the complex fact that the non-Catholic Christians are not completely separated from the Church but are already imperfectly joined to it.

(*d*) The clause 'both are works inspired by the Holy Spirit' is unsuitable. Inspiration refers to holy scripture.

(*e*) The logical order of the text demands that the difference of both works should be mentioned first and be

---

[1] Today this term generally means a propaganda for one's own denomination that works with dishonest means. The expression is explained in the 'Declaration on Religious Liberty'.

followed by the statement that they are not opposed to each other.

(*f*) The beginning of the section 'Hence it is clear' has no causal relation to what has gone before; it should therefore rather start: 'It is, however, clear'. Besides, instead of 'ecumenical action' one should rather say 'ecumenical undertaking' so that the action itself would refer rather more clearly to the grace of the Holy Spirit.

The Secretariat for Unity accepted this *modus* and recommended it to the Fathers, because the proposed new formula was more in accordance with the intention of the decree. The final sentence 'because both proceed from the action of the Holy Spirit' was corrected on 19 November, 1964 to 'for they are both the development of the admirable plan of God'. This formula refers to God's mysterious providence, which comprises natural circumstances and human efforts as well, and especially the working of the Holy Spirit.

There is no doubt that the Catholic faithful engaged in ecumenical activity must be anxious for their separated brethren, must pray for them, share church matters with them, take the first step towards them. They must first of all give their whole-hearted attention to careful consideration of reforms to be made and action to be taken within the Catholic household, if its life is to bear a more faithful and clearer witness to the doctrine and institutions handed down from Christ through the apostles.

The Catholic Church possesses the wealth of the whole of God's revealed truth and all the means of grace: nevertheless, its members do not derive from it all the fervent life that they should. The result is decrease in the radiance with which the face of the Church shines in the eyes of our separated brethren, and of the whole world,

and retarded growth for the kingdom of God. All Catholics, there-
fore, must make Christian perfection their aim[1] and, each in his own
degree, strive for the daily cleansing and renewal of the Church
which carries the lowly and dying state of Jesus in its body[2] until
Christ shall summon it into his presence in all its beauty, no stain,
no wrinkle.[3]

The second version had begun with the statement that
Catholic Christians should undoubtedly be solicitous for the
others through prayer and exchange. A *modus* asked 'others'
to be replaced by 'separated brethren' to clarify who was
meant by 'others'.

The decree continues that Catholic Christians must,
however, be concerned first and foremost about their own
renewal so that the face of the Church might shine more
brightly and the obstacles to the growth of God's kingdom
be removed. The ecumenical action of the Church demands
the renewal of the life of its individual members and its
communities after the example of Jesus Christ. Thus all will
contribute their share assimilating the whole Church ever
more closely to its humble, poor and suffering Lord until he
glorifies it when he comes again.

Here there is no question of 'triumphalism', for the Church
bears the humiliation and passion of Jesus in its pilgrim
members through this earthly time. In God's incomprehensible judgements it is purified and renewed through this
following of Christ. This section corresponds to Chapter
One of the constitution 'On the Church' (n. 8) which
describes the way of the pilgrim Church in weakness and
persecution.

[1] Cf. James 1:4; Rom. 12:1-2.   [2] Cf. 2 Cor. 4:10; Phil. 2:5-8.
[3] Cf. Eph. 5:27.

True, the weaknesses and sins of its members do not deprive the Church of its interior beauty, which is the fruit of Christ's sacrificial love, but they veil, as it were, the face of the Church before the eyes of men. The Council quotes Ephesians 5:27, pointing to the eschatological glorification of the Church, which becomes the heavenly Church at the Second Coming. St Thomas Aquinas comments on this passage: 'The apostle wants to say, as it were: it is not fitting that the immaculate Bridegroom should espouse a bride full of stains. For this reason he represents her to himself as immaculate, here through grace and in the next world through glory. Hence St Paul says: glorious, namely through the glorification of soul and body . . . and without any blemish of impurity. And all this can be understood of the presentation such as it will in future be through glory . . .'[1]

The text of the decree distinguishes holiness as a gift and as a task. The divinely given holiness of the Church is its perpetual gift, the sanctification of its members its constant task.

According to the second version of the text the Church had been endowed with all the riches of the instruments of grace. One suggestion had pointed out that the word instruments was either to be taken as a scholastic technical term or as something mechanical. Hence it should rather be replaced by 'means'. This proposal was accepted, and the final text has 'means of grace'.

While they safeguard unity in essentials, all in the Church should retain a lawful freedom, corresponding to the gift that each has received, in the various kinds of spiritual life and discipline, in the variety of liturgical rites, and even in the theological develop-

[1] In Epist. ad Eph., lect. 8.

ment of revealed truth. In all things they must cultivate charity. By this procedure they will make a demonstration, which is daily more complete, of the catholicity which deserves the name, and of the Church's apostolic character.

On the other hand, it is essential that Catholics be pleased to recognize and set a value on the true Christian possessions which are found among the brethren separated from us and which derive from the common heritage. It is right and salutary to recognize the riches of Christ and the virtues at work in the life of others who bear witness to Christ, at times to the extent of shedding their blood. God is always marvellous and to be marvelled at in his works.

Nor must we disregard the contribution to our own edification which can be made by the effects of the Holy Spirit's grace in our separated brethren. Something which is truly Christian is never opposed to the genuine advantage of the faith, it is, rather, always capable of bringing about a more complete attainment of the very mystery of Christ and the Church.

But the divisions among Christians do constitute a hindrance which prevents the Church's own catholicity from being realized in its fullness, when there are children assigned to it by baptism, yet cut off from its full fellowship. The Church, indeed, finds it more difficult to make her full catholicity a living reality in every respect.

This sacred Synod is pleased to observe the daily increase of the share that the faithful are taking in ecumenical activity. It recommends bishops all over the world to promote this activity energetically and to give it their prudent, personal direction.

True, the catholicity and apostolicity of the Church are gifts integrated into the Church by Christ, but they are also tasks, and the Council admits that unity in necessary things must be joined to freedom in many spheres, including also the elaboration of theology, and must be informed by love so that the Church's catholicity and apostolicity might become perfectly visible.

It is noteworthy that not only the catholicity but also the apostolicity of the Church is more perfectly shown forth by the legitimate variety of rites, the ways of spiritual life, the different forms of canon law and even the various presentations of theology. The reason for this is that the authentic characteristics of the Eastern Churches, for example, derive partly from apostolic traditions, as will be explained in the third chapter.

One Father suggested in his *modus* that the clause on freedom in the theological elaboration of revealed truth had better be left out; for this freedom might be misunderstood and thus the faithful acceptance of revealed truth itself might be endangered. But the Secretariat for Unity pointed out that the schema did not speak of unbounded freedom but of 'lawful freedom', which ruled out this danger.

The saving riches and gifts of Christ which the separated Christians have retained from the common Christian inheritance are expressly recognized. The text of the second version had 'the riches of Christ and the gifts of the Holy Spirit', meaning quite generally the graces given by the Holy Spirit. In Catholic theology, however, the gifts of the Holy Spirit have a special meaning, for in connexion with the Vulgate translation of Isaiah 11:1ff the Schoolmen developed the doctrine of the seven gifts of the Spirit. Catholic theologians are agreed on these gifts, but not on their relation to the theological virtues, their distinction from each other and their number. This may have been the reason for an alteration made on 19 November, 1964, which substituted for the earlier version the words 'the riches of Christ and the virtues at work in the life of others'. The new version connects with the next clause that God is wonderful in his works; for our virtuous acts depend wholly on the grace of God.

Since the earliest days of the Church the witness of blood has taken first place among the works of virtue. The Council mentions the fact that some separated Christians have sealed their witness to Christ with the shedding of their blood. The topicality of this statement can hardly be overlooked.

The second version of the text said that what the Holy Spirit works in the hearts of the separated brethren can also serve for our edification.

An alteration inserted on 19 November, 1964, replaced the words 'by the Holy Spirit' with 'by the effects of the Holy Spirit's grace'; this does not weaken the statement but explains it more accurately: the Holy Spirit produces through his grace all that effects salvation in the soul.

Some *modi* had asked to explain more fully how the faithful were to practise ecumenism. The Secretariat for Unity pointed out that a special *Directorium Oecumenicum* was being worked out which would give more detailed instructions. Individual wishes for more concrete direction could be given neither in the first nor in the second chapter of the decree. In many cases even the *Directorium Oecumenicum* will have to leave the working out of details corresponding to local conditions to the territorial conferences of bishops.

3. Chapter Two: Ecumenism in Practice

CONCERN FOR THE ESTABLISHMENT OF UNITY A MATTER FOR THE WHOLE CHURCH

5. *Concern for the establishment of unity is a matter for the whole Church, faithful and pastors alike. Each individual is affected according to his ability: it may be in day to day Christian living, or in theological and historical research. To a certain extent this anxiety already shows the existence of a brotherly attachment among all Christians. In God's kindness, it is conducive to the completion of full unity.*

This introductory paragraph states that ecumenism concerns the whole Church and occupies each one according to his capacities and opportunities. It is emphasized that despite the existing separations all believers in Christ remain truly brothers and as such are united to one another.

THE RENEWAL OF THE CHURCH

6. *Every renewal of the Church[1] consists essentially in an increase of loyalty to its vocation. This is undoubtedly the reason for the movement towards unity. The Church on its pilgrimage is called by Christ to the continual reformation of which it perpetually*

[1] Cf. Lateran Council V, Sess. XII (1517), Constitution *Constituti:* Mansi 32, 988 B-C.

stands in need, as a human, earthly institution. When occasion offers, correction and due restoration must be made if any carelessness has occurred, as material and temporal conditions change, in the preservation of morals, ecclesiastical discipline or even the manner of formulating doctrine—though this must be carefully distinguished from the deposit of faith.

The ecumenical significance of such renewal is clear. There are various modifications in the life of the Church which are at present working this renewal. Such are the biblical and liturgical movements, the preaching of the Word of God and catechetics, the new forms of religious life, married spirituality, the Church's social teaching and action. They must all be considered as pledges and portents which guarantee the future advance of ecumenism.

In as far as the pilgrim Church is a human and earthly institution it needs constant reform. The constitution *De Ecclesia* also says that the Church must never cease renewing itself through the action of the Holy Spirit. The constant reformation mentioned by the decree refers to the Church 'as a human, earthly institution'. The reform of the Church presupposes that the Christian order of salvation, God's new and eternal covenant with men, can never be replaced by another. Until the second Coming of Christ no new and public revelation is to be expected. The revelation accomplished in Christ and mediated by the apostles cannot be changed or augmented, although it may be ever more fully understood. Nor can there be a higher and more efficacious order of grace than that established by Christ's sacrificial death which is mediated to us by faith and the sacraments. Nor can the apostolic constitution of the Church insofar as it is of divine right undergo a specific change. For this reason the decree says 'as a human, earthly institution'.

The norm according to which the Church is being constantly reformed is holy scripture and the apostolic tradition. The bible is the inspired word of God and has a documentary character. It always renders the voice of the Holy Spirit audible in the Church, so that all the Church's preaching must be nourished by scripture. This is the firm support of the Church which offers believers the strength of faith and the ever-flowing source of their spiritual life. The Church does not govern scripture but serves it and takes it for the rule of its constant reform and renewal, as will be explained by the constitution 'On divine revelation' in chapters two and six.

A number of Fathers raised objections to the clause 'if any carelessness has occurred' (*minus accurate*). They feared that this would not sufficiently express the Church's faithful preservation of the truth of faith. This *modus* was not accepted, because the 'if any carelessness' of the text is very cautious; moreover, it mentions as examples of things that might have to be reformed in certain circumstances, the moral life, Church discipline and the manner of doctrinal exposition, which has to be carefully distinguished from the deposit of faith itself. Here is evident the influence of the opening address of Pope John XXIII on 11 October, 1962 where he distinguished the substance of the ancient doctrine of the deposit of faith from its formulation. The official Latin translation distinguished the deposit of faith from the manner in which the truths contained in it were taught.

A group of a hundred and eleven Fathers considered that the distinction made in the decree required a more detailed explanation. The Secretariat for Unity pointed out that the distinction was sufficiently intelligible. A further *modus*, supported by ninety-two Fathers, expressed the fear that the statements on the reform of the Church could be understood in the sense that in the past there had been no renewals and reforms of the Church. This *modus*, too, did not cause a change in the text, because the decree pronounces a general principle that is valid for every period of Church history while being particularly concerned with the renewal of the Church at the present time, as is shown by the following paragraph, which mentions several movements of renewal in the Church of today which open up hopeful ecumenical aspects.

O. Semmelroth, S.J., says on the constant reform of the Church: 'Hence there is no doubt that despite the Church's continued existence which was promised by the Lord and is guaranteed by the action of his Spirit, it must nevertheless pass through history in constant change ... This is an essential task of the Church, but it is not easily fulfilled. For there are things which, according to the will of Christ must remain and others that can be changed in this way or that throughout the ages; yet both are so close to each other that they cannot simply be separated ... So far one of the most striking results of the Council has certainly been that it has made even those aware of the possibility and necessity of change in the Church's life who had no longer believed in such a thing; on the other hand, over-enthusiastic innovators have realized the difficulties arising from the nature of things or the supernature of the Church.'[1]

[1] Otto Semmelroth, 'Unvergängliches und Wandelbares in der Kirche', in *Lebendiges Zeugnis*, December 1964, 68-70.

THE CONVERSION OF THE HEART

7. There is no genuine ecumenism without an inward conversion. Longings for unity are the product, the ripened fruit, of renewal of the inner life,[1] self-denial and the generous bestowal of charity. We must therefore beseech the divine Spirit for the grace of wholehearted self-denial, humility and gentleness in service, and the open heart of brothers towards other men. 'Here then,' says the apostle of the Gentiles, 'is one who wears the chains in the Lord's service, pleading with you to live as befits men called to such a vocation as yours. You must always be humble, always gentle; patient, too, in bearing with one another's faults, as charity bids, eager to preserve that unity the Spirit gives you whose bond is peace' (Eph. 4:1-3). This exhortation has special significance for those who have been raised to the sacred order for the purpose of continuing the work of Christ; he did not come among us 'to have service done to him; he came to serve others' (Matt. 20:28).

St John's statement has a bearing on faults against unity: 'If we deny that we have sinned, it means that we are treating him as a liar; it means that his word does not dwell in our hearts' (1 John 1:10). Therefore we make a humble plea for the pardon of God and of our separated brethren, as we forgive them that trespass against us.

All Christ's faithful should bear in mind that the value of their efforts to promote, or, rather, to practise the unity of Christians is in proportion to the purity of their desire to order their lives on the gospel. The closer their union with the Father, Word and Spirit, the deeper and readier their ability to make their exchange of brotherly love grow.

[1] Cf. Eph. 4:23.

The constitution *De Ecclesia* also frequently mentions and explains the image of the humble serving Church modelled on the archetype of Jesus Christ and the example of the apostles.

The passage from the First Letter of St John (1 John 1:10) is so generally valid that it can also be applied to the sins against unity which often give rise to divisions. Here Catholic Christians humbly confess their guilt, repeating the petition of the Our Father which expresses forgiveness for those who have trespassed against us. What a change in the attitude of Christians towards one another if we compare this passage with the polemics that had been aggravating the divisions in men's hearts for more than four hundred years!

Forgiveness is asked with that discretion which the decree preserves wherever it mentions the faults and imperfections of the members of the Catholic Church. A certain measure and modesty in these things is a sign of true humility. Though twenty-five Fathers wanted the decree to express itself even more discreetly this was not done, because such caution would have prejudiced the seriousness and sincerity of the confession. Both the subject matter and the tenor of the decree followed Pope Paul VI's confession in his address to the observer delegates on 17 October, 1963.[1]

Eleven Fathers objected that 1 John 1:10 did not refer to sins against unity. Their objections were not accepted either, because, as has already been said, the text makes a general statement which can be applied to sins against unity.

Two Fathers wanted the term conversion to be replaced by another. The Secretariat for Unity replied that this was

[1] The text of this speech may be found in Yves Congar, *Report from Rome II*, London, 1964, pp. 166-70.

an expression constantly used in the theology of the spiritual life for the inner conversion of the heart.

One Father wanted Ephesians 4:1-3 to be left out, because this passage referred to the concord among the faithful in the one Church. He was told that the exhortations of this article are addressed to Catholics.

UNANIMOUS PRAYER

8. Conversion of the heart, holiness of life and prayers, in private and in public, for the unity of Christians must be considered the soul of the ecumenical movement and may rightly be called ecumenism of the spirit.

It is customary for Catholics to have frequent recourse to the prayer for the unity of the Church which the Saviour made with vehemence to the Father the night before he died: 'That they may all be one' (John 17:21).

In certain special circumstances, such as the appointed prayers 'for unity', and ecumenical meetings, the association of Catholics in prayer with their separated brethren is not only lawful but desirable. Such prayers in common are a very effective means of winning the grace of unity; they are an authentic expression of the ties which still attach Catholics to their separated brethren: 'Where two or three are gathered together in my name, I am there in the midst of them' (Matt. 18:20).

The term 'ecumenism of the spirit' goes back to Paul Couturier; it characterizes a whole programme which is described in the first paragraph of this article and called the 'soul of ecumenism'.[1] Eleven Fathers disliked this expression.

[1] P. Michalon points out that several ecumenical suggestions of Abbé Couturier were implemented in the decree 'On Ecumenism': P. Michalon, 'The Abbé Couturier and his Continuing Influence' in *One in Christ* 1 (1965) 6-18.

The Secretariat for Unity replied that the term, though not yet in general use, was nevertheless appropriate and was well explained in the text.

Prayer in common with our separated brethren is recommended especially for the Unity Octave. We might also mention 'services of the Word' which use prayers that may be said by Christians of various denominations without prejudice to their beliefs.

Seven Fathers wanted prayer in common to be treated more cautiously and with certain reservations. They were told that the necessary circumspection was clearly expressed by the words 'in certain special circumstances'.

Three Fathers suggested that the permission of the legitimate ecclesiastical authorities should be mentioned. But this is a matter for the *Directorium Oecumenicum*.

Besides, the recommendation of prayer in common is clearly distinguished from the *communicatio in sacris* which is discussed in the following paragraph.

Sharing in sacred rites, however, is not to be applied indiscriminately as a means to the reunion of Christians. Sharing of this kind is based on two principles: expression of the unity of the Church and sharing in the means of grace. Expression of unity excludes sharing for the most part. The grace to be won sometimes recommends it. In practical application it is for the local episcopal authority to make a prudent decision with reference to circumstances of time, place and person, unless a different decree is made by an episcopal conference following the norm of its own statutes, or by the Holy See.

The Fathers made many proposals concerning the *communicatio in sacris*. Here the decree only established two fundamental principles by which to decide if and when such a *communicatio* is possible or even desirable. The principles themselves were not disapproved of by any of the Fathers.

Seven Fathers wanted a clearer definition of the *communicatio in sacris*. The Secretariat for Unity replied that in theology this concept referred directly to participation in the sacraments and *in obliquo* (indirectly) to participation in any form of worship. The present decree presupposed this terminology. Two Fathers wanted an explanation of both principles as well as an enumeration of cases in which a *communicatio in sacris* would be permissible. But this would have to be reserved to the *Directorium Oecumenicum*. More detailed statements are to be found in article 15 of the first part of Chapter Three in the decree 'On Ecumenism'.

In the second version of the schema this section had ended with the words: 'In practical application it is for the local episcopal authority to make a prudent decision with reference to all the circumstances of time, place and person.' Many Fathers wanted a more exact statement with regard to episcopal authority. No fewer than 212 Fathers wanted to leave the application of the principles to the bishops' conferences, while seventy-six Fathers wanted to reserve this application to the Apostolic Roman See and others to the pope as well as to the bishops' conferences or to the individual bishops. The final text meets all these wishes by an addition which was proposed by the Secretariat for Unity after thorough discussion.

That there can be no eucharistic participation between Catholic and reformed Christians follows necessarily from the absence of the ecclesial unity necessary for it and from the reasons mentioned in article 22 of the decree.

The bishops' conference of the United Evangelical-

Lutheran Church of Germany said in its 'Advice on common events arranged by evangelical and Roman Catholic Christians' issued in January 1965 that evangelical Christians might not take part in the Roman Catholic eucharistic communion. Furthermore: 'As long as there are fundamental differences in the conception of the Church' the 'Advice' continued, 'services in which the evangelical pastor and the Roman Catholic priest take an active part are open to objections in principle. Where a desire for "common services" is expressed the reasons against it must be carefully and honestly thought out. The unity of the Church is represented in the communion of the pulpit and the Lord's Supper. Even without a deeper knowledge of the doctrinal differences, many members of the churches are aware of the fact that the unity of the Church is represented in common worship. They would be confused. We must not feign a communion that does not exist. Services held by the clergy of both churches together easily give the impression of a mere spectacle. It should further be realized that the partners mean something different despite the external similarity of their actions. Finally, the Roman Catholic partner ought also to be considered.'[1]

THE MUTUAL KNOWLEDGE OF THE BRETHREN

9. The mentality of separated brethren must be explored, and this demands a study which combines truth with good will. It is necessary that properly prepared Catholics should improve their knowledge of their brothers' particular teaching and history, spiritual and liturgical life, religious psychology and culture.

[1] 'Ratschläge für interkonfessionelle Begegnungen' in *Missionierende Gemeinde* 12 (1965) 18.

Meetings of the two sides are a great help to this end, especially when their purpose is the discussion of theological questions on a basis of equality, provided that those who take part, with the bishops keeping watch, are real experts. This kind of dialogue will make the true position of the Catholic Church clearer. It will open the way to a better understanding of the intellectual standpoint of our separated brethren and a more adequate exposition to them of our belief.

The expression 'on a basis of equality' (*par cum pari*) is taken verbatim from the Instruction of the Holy Office 'On the Ecumenical Movement' of 20 December, 1949. It means that the partners in the ecumenical dialogue talk to each other on a basis of equality and thus arrive at a better knowledge of their respective positions in doctrine, worship, Church life and spirituality. At the suggestion of one Father the expression 'true position of the Catholic communion' had been changed to 'true position of the Catholic Church'.

ECUMENICAL INSTRUCTION

10. The teaching of sacred theology and other subjects, especially history, should also[1] be treated from an ecumenical viewpoint so that their correspondence to reality may be increasingly exact.

It is of great importance that the bishops and priests of the future should be equipped with a developed theology on these lines, free from the spirit of polemic, especially in matters which have a bearing on the relations of separated brethren with the Catholic Church.

[1] We have supplied this word, which is omitted in the C.T.S. translation translator's note).

The formation the priests receive is the most important factor in the education and spiritual formation which is essential to the aithful and to religious.

Catholics engaged in missionary work in the same area as other Christians must, particularly these days, inform themselves on the problems and benefits to which ecumenism gives rise in their apostolic work.

It is noteworthy that ecumenics are not only one subject among others, but that the ecumenical aspect is to penetrate the whole doctrinal and spiritual instruction.

On the subject of ecumenism and the missions some Fathers wanted an explanation of how the ecumenical attitude should be made effective in the practical missionary work of the various Christian denominations. This question was left to the *Directorium Oecumenicum*.

Two alterations were made in this article: the second version had simply said that theological instruction should be given 'from an ecumenical viewpoint'. 113 Fathers considered this too vague; one Father proposed the insertion of 'also': 'also from the ecumenical viewpoint'. This proposal was accepted, since undoubtedly other points of view must also be taken into account.

The second version said further that the future priests should be well versed in a 'non-polemical theology'. This expression, too, did not please 113 Fathers, and three Fathers suggested changing the adjective 'non-polemical' to the adverb 'not polemically'. This emendation appears in the C.T.S. translation of the final text as 'free from the spirit of polemic'.

The Way in which the Doctrine of Faith is Expressed and Presented

11. The method and manner of presenting Catholic belief should prove no obstacle to dialogue with the brethren. What is absolutely necessary is that the whole teaching be expressed with lucidity. Nothing is so foreign to ecumenism as the false attitude of appeasement which is damaging to the purity of Catholic doctrine and obscures its genuine, established meaning.

At the same time the Catholic belief should be presented with greater depth and accuracy in the manner and the language which will enable even separated brethren to obtain a true grasp of it.

Moreover, Catholic theologians taking part in ecumenical dialogue, while they stick closely to the Church's teaching, should proceed with a love of truth, with charity and humility, when they combine with separated brethren in the scrutiny of divine mysteries. When making comparisons of doctrines, they should remember the existence of an order or 'hierarchy' of the truths of Catholic teaching, since they differ in their connexion with basic Christian belief. The path will thus be open on which this brotherly rivalry will urge all men to a more profound understanding and a clearer demonstration of the unfathomable riches of Christ.[1]

In objecting to a 'false attitude of appeasement', the decree advocates a properly understood, unpolemical discussion of controversial theological issues, penetrated by the ecumenical spirit.

In the general audience of 20 January, 1965, Pope Paul VI has pointed out the importance of this discussion of controversial theological issues if the decree on ecumenism is to be

[1] Cf. Eph. 3:8.

effective. He called the doctrinal differences the greatest difficulty in the way of Christian unity. This obstacle, the pope said, could not be removed by leaving aside or concealing controversial points, by weakening or altering those doctrines of the Catholic Church which the separated brethren do not accept, nor by declaring them unimportant or even denying them. Even well-meaning men were easily tempted to minimalize and put aside certain dogmas that are controversial in order thus to obtain the desired unity. But Christianity, the pope continued, is based on divinely revealed truth, which has been given to us for our salvation, to be accepted, not changed:

> It is good, that the Catholic side acknowledges those good things that are found even today in the inheritance of the Christian churches and denominations separated from the Catholic Church. It is also good that Catholic doctrine is presented in its authentic and essential aspects and that the controversial and inessential ones are left aside. It is good, too, that the controversial points should be presented in a terminology that explains them more accurately and more intelligibly for those who think otherwise. All this belongs to brotherly patience, to apology in the good sense of the word, to charity and the service of truth.
>
> But it would be no good service if statements declared binding and definitive by the magisterium were to be weakened or passed over in silence in order so to overcome the difficulties of doctrinal differences. This does no service to unity, because it raises in the brethren separated from us the suspicion that they are being deceived or else it gives them false hopes. Thus there might arise the fear in

the Church that some seek unity at the cost of truths that are not open to dispute. And so it might be suspected that the dialogue takes place to the detriment of sincerity, faithfulness and truth ... Our partners in the conversations should realize that our attitude is not *a priori* dogmatism, not spiritual imperialism or formal legalism, but perfect obedience to the perfect truth of Christ. The fullness of faith is no jealously guarded treasure, but a brotherly possession always ready; the more we can give it to others, the happier it makes us. It is not ours, but belongs to God and Christ.[1]

The mention of the 'hierarchy of truths' is particularly important; this was absent both from the first and the second versions of the schema 'On Ecumenism'.

Bishop Andreas Pangrazio of Goriza (Italy) had said in the discussion of the first version of the schema:

It is a good thing to enumerate the many ecclesial elements which by God's grace have been preserved in the communities separated from us and which have salutary effects on them. But I frankly confess that it seems to me this enumeration is too 'quantitative', if I may say so; it seems to me to be a mere stringing together. In my opinion some binding factor is required for these individual elements. There should be a centre to which these elements are to be related and without which they cannot be explained. This binding factor and this centre is Christ himself, whom all Christians confess as the Lord of the Church, whom undoubtedly Christians of all communities strive to serve faithfully and who condescends to work

[1] *Osservatore Romano*, 21 January, 1965, p. 1.

wonderful things even in the communities separated from us through his active presence in the Holy Spirit, not, indeed, through the merits of men but solely through the grace of his mercy.

So that the unity already present among Christians, as well as their still existing differences may be properly distinguished, I think it important to consider fully the hierarchical order of the revealed truths through which the mystery of Christ is expressed and of the ecclesial elements by which the Church is established. Even though all revealed truths must be believed with the same divine faith and all constitutive elements of the Church have to be faithfully retained, yet they are not all of the same importance.

There are truths that belong to the order of the end, such as the mystery of the most holy Trinity, of the incarnation of the Word and the redemption, of the divine love and grace towards sinful humanity, of eternal life in the fullness of the kingdom of God, and others.

But there are other truths, which belong to the order of the means of salvation, as for example the truth of the seven sacraments, of the hierarchical structure of the Church, of the apostolic succession and others. These truths concern the means that Christ has given to the Church for her earthly pilgrimage; when this is over they cease.

In fact the doctrinal differences among Christians are less concerned with those truths that belong to the order of the end, and more with those concerning the order of the means, which are undoubtedly subordinate to the former. It may be said that there already exists a unity of Christians in the faith and confession of those truths that belong to the order of the end.

If this distinction according to the hierarchy of truths and elements be explicitly applied, that unity which already exists among all Christians will, I think, become more visible: all Christians are already united in the principal truths of the Christian religion.

During the voting on Chapter Two of the decree, a *modus* was brought in on 7 October, 1964, proposing an addition on the hierarchy of revealed truths after the last word of sentence one of the last paragraph of article 11, *debent* in Latin, (brethren in the present English translation): 'It should be of the greatest importance for the ecumenical dialogue,' the *modus* says, 'that both the truths on which Christians are agreed and the divergent doctrines should be weighed rather than merely enumerated. Though undoubtedly all revealed truths have to be believed with the same divine faith, nevertheless their importance and their "weight" differ according to their relation to salvation history and the mystery of Christ.'

The Secretariat for Unity accepted the proposal and incorporated its content in the final text approved by the Council.

Since the Reformers adhered to the primitive Christian creeds as well as the first four or even six ecumenical Councils, they have preserved the truths of faith stated in these documents as a precious inheritance. They declared these truths, especially the Trinity and the incarnation, to be the 'highest articles of God's majesty' according to the scriptures.

Luther occasionally went even further. Although he blamed the Roman Catholic Church for having falsified the gospel of salvation by its additions, he yet wrote during his struggle with the Anabaptists: 'We confess that under the papacy there has been much, even all Christian treasure, and that it also came to us from there, because we confess that in the papacy there is the true holy scripture, the true baptism, the true sacrament of the altar, the true key to the forgiveness of sins, true preaching office, true catechism such as the Ten Commandments, the articles of faith and the Our Father . . . I say that under the pope there is true Christianity, even the model of Christianity and many devout great saints . . . We are not fanatics like the sectarians who reject everything to do with the papacy, for thus we would also reject Christianity, with all it has in Christ. . . .'[1] Melanchthon affirmed in a letter to Cardinal Campeggio of 3 July, 1530 that nothing had caused the followers of the Reformation to be hated more than their steadfast defence of the doctrines of the Roman Church.[2] This, too, is an allusion to the Reformers' fight against the sectarians in which they defended essentials of Catholic doctrine.

In the Schmalkaldic Articles of February 1537, which most clearly express Luther's opposition to the Roman Catholic Church, it is expressly stated that there is no controversy with the Catholic Church on the doctrine of the Trinity and on Christology. The four articles treating these doctrines that Catholics and Protestants have in common are entitled: 'On the highest articles of the divine Majesty'

---

[1] *Sendschreiben an zwei Pfarrherren von der Wiedertaufe*, 1528, in the Weimar edition of Luther's work vol. 26, 257 f.

[2] CR II, 168 f.

(*De summis articulis divinae majestatis*). No one will dispute that these doctrines actually rank highest among all the truths of revelation. Luther says of them: 'These articles are not a matter of dispute and controversy, since both parties profess them. Hence it is not necessary to discuss them still further.'

Present-day evangelical theologians hold different views on the retention of the ancient creeds by the Reformers, as is clear from the diametrically opposed opinions of Werner Elert and Gerhard Ebeling. Both Catholic and Protestant theologians have emphasized that there are differences between the Catholic and Protestant interpretation of Christology and soteriology. The decree 'On Ecumenism' mentions these differences in article 20 and asks for discussion.

CO-OPERATION WITH THE SEPARATED BRETHREN

12. All Christians must make a proclamation before all nations of their belief in God, who is One and Three, in the Son of God incarnate, our Lord and Redeemer. By their common effort, with respect for each other, they must bear witness to the hope which we have, and which does not bring disappointment. Since modern times are the witness of the commencement of extensive co-operation in social work, all men are called to a community of labour. All the more reason then for those who believe in God to co-operate, and most of all Christians, since they carry the special distinction of Christ's name. The co-operation of all Christians is the living expression of the attachment which already connects them; it puts the countenance of Christ the servant[1] in a clearer light. This co-operation has already been initiated in many countries; it must be

[1] We have supplied the words 'the servant' (Latin text: *Christi Servi*) omitted in the C.T.S. translation (translator's note).

increasingly perfected, especially in areas where social and technological evolution is the order of the day: co-operation in the correct evaluation of the dignity of the human person, in the promotion of peace, in the application of gospel sociology, in securing the advance of the sciences and the arts in a Christian spirit, in the provision of every kind of cure for the troubles of our day—famine, disasters, illiteracy, want, housing shortage, inequality in the distribution of goods. Such co-operation will enable all who believe in Christ to learn how to reach a better understanding and appreciation of each other, to learn too how the way may be opened to the unity of Christians.

We must not stop short at dialogue. However important mutual knowledge and understanding, we must live and work together with our non-Catholic brothers and sisters. In the long run our encounter must also lead to common action. Catholic Christians are prepared to do in common with other Christians whatever can be done in this way. That is already a good deal.

The Council mentions in the first place the common witness to faith in the most holy Trinity and the incarnation of the Son of God, our Lord and Saviour, as well as the common confession of the eschatological hope of Christendom. It is, moreover, made clear that the collaboration of Christians in the spheres of scholarship, art and culture, of social progress and world peace, has its own *Christian* characteristic which distinguishes it from all other forms of co-operation which are founded only on the natural law. Hence this collaboration, too, manifests an already existing interior union of those who believe in Christ and by their active love show forth the image of the Servant, traced by Isaiah.

Several bishops wanted the reference to the Servant to be made clearer. Twelve Fathers proposed 'the face of Christ, the servant of his Father', two: 'the face of Christ, the servant of Yahweh', or: 'the face of Christ who came not to be served but to serve' and another one: 'the face of Christ the redeemer of mankind'.

These proposals were not accepted because the existing text pointed sufficiently clearly to the Servant prophesied by Isaiah.

One Father feared that the mention of the underdeveloped countries might give offence to certain nations. The text remained unchanged, because it only reminds Christians of their responsibility for these countries.

Three Fathers wanted mentioned the difficulties that are caused by the proselytizing propaganda of certain sects; another wanted something to be said against proselytism and indifferentism. These suggestions can be considered in the *Directorium Oecumenicum*.

Thirty-six Fathers asked for a reference to the Ecumenical Directories to be worked out by the individual bishops, conferences for their respective territories. The Secretariat for Unity replied that in his *relationes* and Council speeches, Cardinal Bea had several times spoken of the general *Directorium Oecumenicum*, which will be drawn up by the Secretariat for Christian Unity. It would be difficult to mention this or special individual directories in the decree.

Where the decree mentions co-operation in applying the gospel to social questions it might seem as if the differences between Catholics and Protestants with regard to moral and social teaching were overlooked; but this difference is mentioned in article 23, which recommends a dialogue on these matters.

4. Chapter Three: The Churches and Ecclesial Communities Separated from the Apostolic See of Rome

THIS title comprises the Eastern as well as the Western communities separated from us. Questions of the application of the term Church to the individual Christian denominations are left to the theologians for further discussion. The Eastern Churches are always called 'Churches' in the theological sense. They are treated in a separate section so as to distinguish them from the Western Churches and ecclesial communities. This distinction does not prejudice the unity of the ecumenical problem, but it results from the special characteristics of the various communities. The Eastern Churches differ essentially from those of the Reformation and precisely in the ecclesiological sphere, as the Dominican theologian Le Guillou has once more proved in his essay 'Fragen zur Zukunft des Ökumenismus' (Questions on the Future of Ecumenism).[1]

On the Protestant side it has been said that the decree 'On Ecumenism' judges the churches and communities separated from the Catholic Church according to the number of ecclesial elements they share with the latter. In his Rome press conference of 11 November, 1964 Dr Lukas Vischer

[1] In *Istina* 1964, 7-24.

said: 'The one and only Church of Christ is at the centre, building bridges for the separated brethren. It looks at the non-Roman churches from the point of view of their relation to the Roman Catholic Church. It addresses first of all those that seem to be particularly near to it and then gradually turns its attention to those churches that seem to have less in common with it. This ecumenical method may be pictured as concentric circles. The Roman Catholic Church is at the centre and sees the non-Roman churches outside its frontiers at a greater or lesser distance.'

This interpretation does not completely correspond to the perspectives of the decree 'On Ecumenism'. For the decree regards Christ as the only centre on which depend both the Catholic Church and the churches and ecclesial communities separated from it in all the means of salvation they possess, however different their ecclesial situation. Thus the Holy Spirit, who is the Spirit of Christ, already creates the actual, even though imperfect unity of a graduated community. The Catholic Church does not take the place of Christ, but obeys his will to create the perfect unity of this community. This is the intention of the decree, which for this reason teaches the necessity of a constant renewal of the Church from the Spirit of Jesus Christ.

The schema also implies that the institutional perfection of the Church is historically encumbered by the imperfections, faults and sins of its members. Bishop Stefan László of Eisenstadt said in the Council hall: 'The Church is called a pilgrim Church because in all the misery of this life its people is not without guilt and sin. In this the New Testament people of God continues the people of the Old Testament. Often the people wants to follow the way of the Lord, but unhappily it goes astray time and again; it wants to be faithful, but again and again it is found unfaithful; it wants to live holy and just in the grace of God, but time and again it appears sinful, incurring God's wrath . . . When, as early as at the sixteenth Synod of Carthage, all Novatianist and Donatist, that is to say all triumphalist and idealistic, ecclesiology was excluded, the Fathers of the Synod declared that even the saints in the Church should confess themselves to be sinners and say not only from humility, but in accordance with the truth, "forgive us our trespasses".[1]

Here we shall remember the exhortation of St Paul, who impressed on the church at Corinth that in the Old as well as in the New Covenant the guilt of the faithful prevents the institutional means of salvation from taking effect. Just as in the Old Covenant the people of God received in its own way a baptism and a spiritual food and yet became guilty and was not allowed to see the promised land, so also the people of the New Testament is threatened by sin and by the loss of salvation.[2] The church of Corinth should ask itself whether it really lives according to faith and baptism in order to resemble Christ. If it were incapable of repentance it would have to fear being rejected at the judgement.[3]

Similarly today, too, many members of a Catholic diocese, which is institutionally a complete, individual church possessing all the means of salvation, might through their own fault live according to the gospel only in a rudimentary and faulty way, while a non-Catholic ecclesial community, even though without some ecclesial elements, might possess

---

[1] Cf. Denz. 106-8.   [2] Cf. 1 Cor. 10:1-13.
[3] Cf. 2 Cor. 12:19-13:10.

many Christians who follow the gospel more deeply and sincerely. True, in the Catholic Church there is no 'substantial unfaithfulness to the divine intention of its Author', but there may be unfaithfulness of its members to the demands of the gospel. Hence the Council exhorts Catholics to constant repentance and asks them joyfully to admit the good that the Holy Spirit works in the separated brethren and which may contribute to our edification.[1] In several passages the decree 'On Ecumenism' has described in a positive way the fruits of the workings of the Holy Spirit in the Churches and ecclesial communities separated from us. It is generally admitted that the ecumenical movement which has been called forth by the grace of the Holy Spirit first appeared in the non-Catholic Christian world, even though in the Catholic Church, too, there have always been efforts to promote the unity of Christians.

We gladly agree with Dr Lukas Vischer who draws attention to the simple but supremely important truth that the Holy Spirit himself is the author of all true reform and renewal: 'The renewal', Dr Vischer says, 'leads to freedom and joy, but it always also contains the element of shame. Joy and gratitude for the renewal are the greater, purer and stronger the more they are accompanied by this shame. It is important to see this, since such an insight can unite the churches. For then their renewal will not be regarded as a triumph carrying everything before it. The dialogue will become neither a spectacular self-advertisement nor a cramped self-defence. Feelings of prestige and superiority which today occasionally darken the ecumenical scene can be overcome. The discussions of the Council and the text

[1] Article 4.

"On Ecumenism" have shown something of this new spirit which, we hope, will imbue the ecumenical style that will gradually emerge after the promulgation of the text.'[1]

THE TWO GREAT DIVISIONS OF THE CHURCH

13. We now direct our attention to the rents in the seamless garment of Christ, under two main headings.

The first kind occurred in the East in the conflict over the dogmatic formulae of the Councils of Ephesus and Chalcedon and, at a later date, with the breaking off of communion between the Eastern Patriarchates and the See of Rome.

The second type arose in the West more than four centuries later; they are covered by the general title of the Reformation. Since then, many communions based on nationality or common belief have been separated from the Roman See. The Anglican Communion has a special place among those which continue to retain, in part, Catholic traditions and structure.

There are considerable differences between these various divisions as a result of the place and time of their origin and, in particular, because of serious disputes over the Church's belief and organization.

For this reason, the sacred Synod, without belittling the different situations of the various Christian groups and without disregard for the ties which have survived the separation between them, makes its decision to put forward the following considerations for the prudent practice of ecumenism.

The intention of this whole chapter is made clear in a brief introduction. It will discuss the great churches and ecclesial communities separated from us in order to give

[1] Rome press conferences, 11 November, 1964.

guidance to the ecumenical activities of Catholic Christians.

The divisions of the Church fall into two main categories, those of the East and those of the West, both affecting the seamless robe of Christ. The latter expression is frequently used in the Eastern tradition.

Two Fathers thought that this image should not be used, since the robe of Christ could not be divided. The Secretariat for Unity replied that it was clear to everyone that the separation here did not refer to the image, the robe of Christ, but to what it signified, namely the unity of Christians in the one Church.

The decree mentions the great difference between the divisions of the East and those of the West during the Reformation and the following centuries, pointing especially to the ecclesiological differences between Eastern and Reformed Christianity. For this reason Chapter Three is divided into two main parts, the first of which deals with the Eastern Churches, while the subject of the second is the Reformation and post-Reformation churches and ecclesial communities of the West separated from the Apostolic See of Rome. The Council wants to distinguish but not to separate the treatment of both parts and points out especially the common elements of both. The ecumenical problem affects all Christendom and this has always to be taken into account despite the necessary distinctions.

After the Council of Ephesus (431) the Chaldaic Christians, called Nestorians by their opponents, separated from the universal Church; in India they were called 'Thomas Christians' and spread also to China. A further separation took place after the Council of Chalcedon in 451, when the non-Chalcedonian churches separated from the Catholic

Church because they opposed the doctrine of the two natures of Christ. Today these Churches (Copts and Abyssinians) no longer teach monophysitism. On the contrary, both in their ancient liturgy and their preaching they bear witness that Christ unites his divine and his human nature in his one divine Person. In his encyclical *Sempiternus Rex* of 8 September, 1951 Pius XII had already stated that the dogmatic differences are apparent and verbal rather than real. The decree rightly says that the early Eastern divisions of the Church originated through contesting the dogmatic formulae of Ephesus and Chalcedon. Both the afore-mentioned Eastern Churches have sent observer delegates to the Second Vatican Council.

The decree then mentions the great separation of the Eastern Churches that started in 1054 and was due to the breaking off of ecclesiastical communion between the Eastern patriarchs and the Roman See. This division was not caused by dogmatic differences, as is explicitly stated in the *relatio* on this part of the schema. One Father proposed not to mention the patriarchates and to speak simply of the breaking off of ecclesiastical communion. The Secretariat for Unity, however, considered it necessary to say in what the breaking off of the communion consisted. For this is a matter of the Eastern Churches with their patriarchates, and it is a historical fact that the so-called Eastern schism took place in the way stated by the decree.

Two Fathers had doubts about the date of the Western divisions. They wanted the words 'after more than four centuries' to be left out. They evidently had in mind the medieval divisions which originated before the Reformation. But here the decree meant to mention only the *great* divisions of the Church and incidentally, the date given also covers the predecessors of the Reformation in the later middle ages.

The second version of the decree had stated that other divisions had taken place 'in just this Western Church'. This was changed on 19 November, 1964 to: 'in the West', which corresponds to the immediately preceding 'in the East'. But perhaps this change was also influenced by the view that not all the causes of the Reformation were strictly ecclesiastical.

The decree calls the separated churches in the West communions, an expression which comprises churches as well as communities. Hence the suggestion of one Father that communions should be replaced by communities was not followed.

Forty-three Fathers, many of them from England, objected to the terminology of the second version, according to which these communities had 'separated themselves' from the Roman See. This could be interpreted as putting all the blame for the separation on one side, whereas the question of guilt should here be left aside altogether. It further did not correspond to the facts that all these communions had rejected Rome. Perhaps the Fathers had in mind the events under Henry VIII as much as the principle *Cuius regio, eius religio* followed on the continent at that time, according to which the princes determined the religion of their subjects.

This proposal was accepted, and the final text said simply that these communities were separated.

The second version contained a special mention of the Anglican Communion. This expression is in general use for the Church of England and has become the accepted term. It is generally recognized in the ecumenical movement that despite their affinities, Anglicanism must be distinguished from continental Protestantism. The decree does justice to this at least in this passage. Originally it had used the term 'is pre-eminent' among those communities in which Catholic traditions and structures partly continue; but some of the Fathers feared that other communions might take the word 'pre-eminent' as discriminating against themselves. One of the Fathers asked why the Anglican Communion should be superior in this matter to the Old Catholic Church. Every semblance of passing judgement ought to be avoided, hence one should simply say 'has a special place'. The Secretariat for Unity recommended this proposal for acceptance by the Council, it therefore appears in the final decree.

This article points out the differences in the divisions and mentions the special doctrines regarding faith and the structure of the Church. One *modus* proposed to replace 'ecclesiastical structure' by 'constitution'. This proposal was not accepted, because the constitution of the Church is necessarily an object of faith and cannot therefore be distinguished from the other objects of faith, whereas an ecclesiastical structure can in some way be so distinguished.

I. Special Consideration of the Eastern Churches.

The Attitude and History Proper to the Easterns

14. *For many centuries the Churches of the East and West followed their own path yet were linked in the fellowship of brothers, in faith and sacramental life. By common consent, the Roman See was in control should disagreements over faith or discipline arise between them. Among other important matters, the*

sacred Synod takes pleasure in reminding all men that many particular local Churches are flourishing in the East, including the patriarchal Churches which hold the leading position, and several of them boast an apostolic origin. From that time onwards, there has prevailed among the Eastern Christians a concern and care for the preservation of the family relationship in the fellowship of faith and charity that should exist in local churches, for they are sisters; it still prevails in our day.

There is, likewise, no ignoring the fact that, from the beginning, the Churches of the East have been in possession of a treasury from which the Western Church has borrowed heavily in the way of liturgical practice, spiritual tradition and juridical organization. Nor must it be considered unimportant that it was at ecumenical Councils held in the East that the fundamental dogmas of the Christian belief, in the Trinity and the Word of God made flesh of the Virgin Mary, were defined. The preservation of this belief has cost and still costs that Church much suffering.

The apostolic heritage has had various forms of modified acceptance: from the very beginning of the Church, it has had a different development in various places as a result of variety of character and living conditions. With the failure of mutual understanding and charity, not to mention external causes, all this has given divisions their purchase.

For this reason, the sacred Synod calls upon all men to give due consideration to the special character of the birth and development of the Churches of the East and to the character of the relations which existed between them and Rome before the separation; they must be correct in their appraisal of these matters. The exhortation is especially directed to men who make it their aim to further the restoration of full communion which is desired between the Eastern Churches and the Catholic Church. If these points are carefully *kept in mind, it will make a supreme contribution to the proposed dialogue.*

For more than a thousand years the special theological presentation, liturgy, canon law and spirituality proper to the Eastern Churches existed peacefully together in union with the more or less different Western ways. A number of Eastern Churches were founded directly by an apostle, for example Ephesus by St John, Corinth by St Paul.

The ancient patriarchal Churches claim to have been founded by an apostle or by a disciple of the apostles, for example Antioch by St Peter, Alexandria by St Mark, Jerusalem by St James and Constantinople by St Andrew. Because the Roman Church was founded by St Peter and St Paul it is the patriarchal Church of the West, and because of the authority of the princes of the apostles it is simply called the Apostolic See.

The second version of the schema had stated that 'in the East many particular local churches derive their origin from the apostles themselves'. One Father wanted mention made here of the patriarchal Churches. The Secretariat for Unity therefore proposed an enlarged text: 'That many particular local Churches are flourishing in the East, including the patriarchal Churches which hold the leading position, and several of them boast an apostolic origin.'

The Secretariat for Unity gave the following reasons for this insertion:

1. Although the patriarchates had been mentioned in the preceding article, so far they had not been treated in the special consideration of the Eastern Churches. Now the patriarchates are so important for Eastern ecclesiology that

it would be unintelligible if they were not explicitly mentioned.

2. The proposed insertion does not change the meaning of the existing text, which presupposes the existence of the patriarchal Churches.

3. The new addition corresponds to the dogmatic constitution *De Ecclesia* which treats in the same sense of the patriarchal Churches in article 33 and note 37.

An alteration added on 19 November, 1964 concerned only the last words of the addition, saying that not a few of these Churches 'derive their origin from the apostles themselves'. Instead the final text now says that they 'glory in their apostolic origin'. This alteration in no way questions the direct apostolic origin of many Eastern and patriarchal Churches, it only gives more weight to the complicated historical problems of the origin of some Eastern Churches, whose direct apostolic origin is asserted by a venerable tradition but is difficult to prove historically.

The decree uses the terms 'particular local Churches' in the same sense in which article 23 of the constitution *De Ecclesia* speaks of local Churches of apostolic origin. The proposal of one of the Fathers to characterize these Churches as special 'rites' could not be accepted, because there are local Churches founded by the apostles that have no special rite; the Secretariat for Unity gave the Churches of Thessalonica and Corinth as examples.

While all Western Catholic Churches derive their origin from the Roman Apostolic Church, in the East there are several Churches founded directly by the apostles, and these in their turn founded other local Churches. Through their origin the Churches founded by the apostles in the East are sister Churches, not daughter Churches, of the Roman Church.

The second version of the schema had said on the subject of all Churches being led by the successor of the apostle Peter: 'While according to common consent (*iuxta communem consensum*) the Roman See took the lead.' Nine Fathers proposed to say instead 'by common consent' (*communi consensu*) in order to remove the misunderstanding that the Eastern Churches had recognized the primacy only according to a common agreement. This proposal was accepted. The decree does not mean to say that the Roman See took the lead because of a common agreement, but that in those days there existed a consensus of opinion by which all actually acknowledged the Roman primacy and its power of leadership. In other words, the decree treats of the historical fact of the consensus, not of the theological basis of the origin of the primacy of the Roman See.

The second version had stated that from the beginning the Eastern Churches had possessed 'a treasure of their own'. One Father observed that this liturgical and theological treasure was not the special property of the Eastern Churches insofar as they were separated from the Western Churches, but that the Eastern Churches had preserved this treasure from the time when East and West were still united in one Church. As the term 'proper' could perhaps give rise to misunderstanding it was left out in the final text.

The text says that the Western Church has borrowed heavily from the treasury of the Eastern Church. Eleven Fathers proposed to speak in the plural not only of the Eastern, but also of the Western Church, suggesting 'the other Churches'. This proposal was not accepted for the following reasons:

1. The Churches of the East are not opposed to some other Churches but to the one Church of the West.

2. The Western Church means the whole of Western Catholic Christendom. This has taken over much from the Eastern Churches, which also applies to the non-Catholic Western Churches and ecclesial communities.

3. In the East there are several Eastern Apostolic Sees, whereas in the West there is only the one Apostolic Roman See.

The decree mentions the witness of suffering that the Eastern Churches bear to the truths of faith defined by the earlier Councils. These Churches have suffered and are still suffering. The persecution is directed not only against individual believers but often enough directly against the Church as an institution, and the faithful suffer nearly always as members of the one Christian Church. Among the truths to which these Churches testify the second version also mentions the incarnation of the Son of God from the virginal Mother of God. A correction inserted on 19 November changed the words 'of the Virgin Mother of God' to 'of the Virgin Mary'. This alteration is a matter of style.

The second version of the schema said that, apart from external reasons, the differences between East and West became the occasion of the separation owing to the lack of mutual understanding and love. One Father observed that there were other reasons, too, which the decree, which suffered from an inferiority complex, simply did not dare to name. The Secretariat for Unity replied that history showed quite clearly that external reasons and differently interpreted traditions were at the root of the separation. Moreover, the Council did not intend to give all the reasons for the separation in systematic order: other, inner reasons were not excluded by the formulation of the decree.

Another Father wanted the words 'with the failure of mutual understanding and charity' to be left out. He did not give a reason, but like the first-named Father he probably considered the text an over-simplification.

In the last section of this article, which deals with the restoration of full communion between the Eastern Churches and the Catholic Church, the words 'full communion' were qualified by 'desired', on 19 November, 1964. Thus full ecclesial communion is emphasized as the object of our longing as had already been said several times in the decree.

The Liturgical and Spiritual Tradition of the Easterns

15. Everyone is familiar with the great love which Eastern Churches put into the performance of the sacred liturgy, especially the celebration of the eucharist, the Church's life-spring and pledge of the glory that is to come. That is where the faithful join their bishop and, through the Son, the Word made flesh, who has suffered and entered his glory, with the outpouring of the Holy Spirit, have access to God the Father and attain fellowship with the Blessed Trinity, for they are made 'to share the divine nature' (2 Peter 1:4). The celebration of the Lord's eucharist in the individual Churches builds up the Church of God and makes it grow,[1] *while the practice of concelebration makes their fellowship manifest.*

[1] Cf. St John Chrysostom, *Homily XLVI on John:* PG 59, 260-2.

Starting from the sacramental character of the mystery of the Church as it is developed in Chapter Three of the constitution *De Ecclesia* (article 26), the decree has shown the eucharist as the source of the Church's life and the earnest of the future glory. Through the eucharist the faithful united to their bishop realize in the Holy Spirit a communion with the persons of the most holy Trinity. With this formula the Council tries to present the conception of the eucharist familiar to the Easterns. The celebration of the eucharist builds up the individual Churches into the Church; this is a sure doctrine of scripture (1 Cor. 10:17) and of tradition, which has been expounded in the West especially by St Augustine, in the East by St Cyril of Jerusalem and St John Chrysostom. In the dogmatic constitution *De Ecclesia* this effect of the eucharist is mentioned in Chapter One article three.

Several Fathers had objections to the sentence that in these individual Eastern Churches the Church is built up through the celebration of the eucharist. One Father feared that the whole motive of ecumenism was destroyed by this assertion. Moreover, it could not be said that through the celebration of the eucharist in the separated Eastern Churches the Church is built up and grows in the same way as through the celebration of the eucharist in the Catholic Church. Hence the 'built up' should be qualified by the words 'in a certain true manner' to point out the difference.

The Secretariat for Unity replied that the text in no way destroyed the motive for ecumenism. It was rather a question of recognizing the authentic sacramental treasure of the Eastern Churches, and such a recognition belonged to the essence of true ecumenism. It was also not quite intelligible why the building up of the individual church in the Catholic Church through the celebration of the eucharist as such should be different in the Orthodox Churches. The actually existing difference was due rather to the accompanying circumstances which belong more to the canonical than to the specifically sacramental order. Nor did the text assert that the Church is built up through the celebration of the eucharist alone. All that was said was that the celebration of the true eucharist truly contributes to the building up of the Church. Moreover, the effect of the eucharist was not diminished by the mere fact that someone erred in good faith.

In this worship of the liturgy Eastern Christians extol Mary, ever a virgin, with hymns of great beauty. It was, after all, the ecumenical Synod at Ephesus that made the solemn proclamation of Mary as the most holy Mother of God, to secure for Christ an appropriate and true recognition as Son of God and Son of Man, as the scriptures show him. They also, in the liturgy, sing the praises of many other saints, including the Fathers of the universal Church.

The documents of the Council frequently refer to the Eastern Churches' traditional veneration of the 'all-holy Mother of God' and the Fathers of the early Church, both here and in the constitution *De Ecclesia* in chapter eight, article sixty-nine.

The orthodox Metropolitan Seraphim says: 'It is a consoling sign that the inner unity of both Churches has never been completely lost; that, despite the external separation, the now separated Churches of East and West venerate the same saints in such great number; and this in addition to such features in common as the same succession, the same holy scriptures and the close affinity in the administration of the holy sacraments. Finally, the relationship between the Churches of the East and of the West is manifest also in the Orthodox and Catholic popular piety that has developed in the course of history and is expressed in the same way in both Churches, in the veneration of the Mother of God and the saints, in the veneration of holy images and relics, in fasts and pilgrimages and in the esteem for the consecrations and blessings of the Church.'[1]

These Churches, for all their separation, are in possession of true sacraments, notably the priesthood and the eucharist, in virtue of the apostolic succession. This possession of theirs keeps them connected to us by the closest degree of kinship. Given appropriate circumstances, therefore, and the approval of ecclesiastical authority, some sharing in sacred rites is not only possible but advisable.

The principles for the *communicatio in sacris* pronounced in article 8 of Chapter Two of this decree are here applied to the Eastern Churches not in complete ecclesial communion with the Apostolic Roman See. Their valid celebration of the eucharist and their preservation of the other sacraments create a relationship with ourselves which in certain cases make the *communicatio in sacris*—which here embraces participation in the eucharistic celebration and reception of the sacraments—not only possible but even advisable. The decree 'On Eastern Catholic Churches' treats of this in articles 26-9 and advises consultation of the hierarchy of these Churches which are separated from us. Without the consent of these hierarchies even a limited *communicatio in sacris* will neither be possible in the long run nor as a rule advisable.

Seventy-nine Fathers had objections to the unconditional

[1] Metropolitan Seraphim, *Die Ostkirche*, Stuttgart 1950, 138 f.

statement 'in virtue of the apostolic succession'. They drew attention to the fact that the apostolic succession in the full sense of the term presupposes more than merely valid episcopal consecration. Formally understood it existed only in communion with the successor of Peter.

The theological manuals distinguish between 'material apostolic succession' obtained by valid episcopal consecration and 'formal apostolic succession' which includes communion with the Apostolic Roman See. The Secretariat for Unity was aware of the fact that the perfect apostolic succession includes complete communion with the successor of Peter; but it considered it very difficult to explain these details. It said that it was clear from the context that here it was a question of valid sacramental powers which had been received from the apostles and had never been lost even after the separation. For the same reason proposals from eleven Fathers which wanted to replace the words 'in virtue of the apostolic succession' by others such as 'in virtue of the sacramental succession' or 'in virtue of non-interrupted succession' or 'in virtue of episcopal succession' were rejected.

Another proposal of one Father, to replace 'the closest degree of kinship' by 'no small degree of kinship' was also rejected. The Secretariat for Unity regarded this as an incorrect weakening of the sense intended by the text. For the Council was especially concerned to emphasize the very close relationship between these Churches and the Catholic Church, through which a certain *communicatio in sacris* becomes possible and even advisable.

Several Fathers raised objections to the *communicatio in sacris* proposed in the decree. The majority of their proposals will be treated in the *Directorium Oecumenicum*. But in order to meet their wishes the words 'with the approval of ecclesiastical authority' were inserted. The authority here referred to is that mentioned in Chapter Two article 8 of the decree.

The directives of the decree on the *communicatio in sacris* with the Eastern Churches are of great importance. Many Fathers had already made similar proposals in the Council hall. In the East the *communicatio* mentioned in the decree had long been practised in one way or another and could be traced back to an early tradition. The first schema 'On the Church' worked out by the preparatory Theological Commission had contained similar proposals, which have now been included in the decree 'On the Catholic Eastern Churches' (articles 26-9).

The restoration of complete ecclesial communion with the Eastern Churches has not only to be prepared by theological dialogue, however necessary this may be; it needs also the practical expression of our close affinity with these Churches. If we have the common services mentioned in the decree and have that complete confidence in one another which avoids every form of dishonest 'proselytism', the laity on both sides will happily realize how closely they are related to each other and how much they still have in common. This points to the complete ecclesial communion which we hope the Holy Spirit will provide.

In the East one finds, moreover, a wealth of spiritual traditions formed chiefly by monasticism. Monastic spirituality has had a flourishing existence in the East ever since the glorious days of the Fathers. It has spread to the West from the East and has been the source and wellspring of the formation of the religious life among the Latins, and has repeatedly been a force of re-invigoration. This is the reason why Catholics are earnestly recommended to have frequent recourse to the spiritual treasury of the Eastern Fathers, it catches a man up entirely in divine contemplation.

The Orthodox Metropolitan Seraphim says: 'The monastic Rules of St Basil, this great work of ancient Christian wisdom, were transmitted to the West in the translation of Rufinus. In early times monasteries following the Rule of St Basil were founded in Southern Italy, Sicily and Spain. At the time of the iconoclasts many Greek monks emigrated to the West. True, there the Rule of St Basil was soon replaced by the Rule of St Benedict, the great patriarch of Western monasticism, who is venerated as a saint in the Eastern Church also. But, as St Benedict himself says, the Rule of St Basil was one of his principal sources. He recommended in his Rule the reading of the *Collationes Patrum* (conversations with the most revered Egyptian hermits) by John Cassian . . . . Later Cassian founded two monasteries on the Eastern pattern near Marseilles. His monasticism greatly influenced the Benedictine monasticism of the middle ages. How great this influence was may be seen from the fact that St Thomas Aquinas, who had himself been educated by the Benedictines, kept the *Collationes* on his desk for frequent use.'[1]

The statement of the decree that the religious institutes of the Latins 'received ever new vigour' from the monastic spirituality of the East was questioned by one of the Fathers

---

[1] 'Die Ostkirche', loc. cit. 134. Jean Daniélou makes an important statement: 'St Benedict himself remains a saint of a very Eastern type', *Nouvelle Histoire de l'Eglise*, vol. 1: *Des origines à S. Grégoire le Grand*. Par J. Daniélou et H. I. Marrou, Paris 1963, 483.

who said that this statement was not in complete accordance with the truth. For, he said, in the West there originated new religious rules which were quite different from those of Eastern monasticism as well as from the earlier monasticism of the West.

The Secretariat of Unity replied: Our text does not maintain that the whole monastic spirituality of the West sprung from Eastern monasticism. It is sufficient that the monastic spirituality of the West should have strongly been influenced by Eastern monasticism at some time. This is always true, even today. For this spirituality that had first flourished in the East is still vigorous and exercises its influence even with us.

Recognition, respect, preservation and encouragement—everyone must know the importance of these attitudes with regard to the liturgical and spiritual heritage of Eastern Christians, if a loyal guard is to be kept on the fullness of the Christian tradition, and the reconciliation of Eastern and Western Christians is to be accomplished.

One Father wanted the spiritual patrimony of the Easterns to be expressly described as a Catholic inheritance which they had preserved. The Secretariat for Unity replied that article 17 of the decree said that the inheritance which remained active in the separated Churches throughout the centuries belongs to the full catholicity and apostolicity of the Church.

Another Father proposed that the Easterns should be asked to study the patrimony of the Western Church in their turn. Though this proposal was considered opportune it was thought to be less suitable for this decree.

THE DISCIPLINE PROPER TO THE EASTERNS

16. Furthermore, the Churches of the East had, from earliest times, always followed their own rules which had the authorization of the Fathers, the Synods, and ecumenical Synods at that. Variety in practice and custom is no obstacle to the Church's unity; on the contrary, it is an embellishment and it makes no slight contribution to the fulfilment of her mission (cf. supra). The sacred Synod, therefore, hopes to remove all doubt with the announcement that the Churches of the East, with the requirements of the unity of the whole Church in mind, have every opportunity to govern themselves by their own rules which are, after all, more suited to the mentality of their faithful and better adapted to securing the good of their souls. Thoroughgoing observance of this traditional principle—it has not always been maintained—is one of the essential preliminary conditions for reunion.

The preservation and application of the canon law proper to the Eastern Churches is a fundamental principle of the preservation or restoration of the unity between the Eastern and Western Churches. This principle, frequently stated by the popes, is now solemnly proclaimed by the Council. One of the Fathers thought it too little to say that 'variety in practice and custom is an embellishment to the Church'. He proposed to say instead that this variety manifests 'a richer life of the Church' or 'its vitality'. For it was not a matter of an external increase of beauty but of its inner vitality which was manifested in many ways.

The Secretariat for Unity answered:

1. St Augustine already uses the image of the queen, the consort of the king, who is dressed in many-coloured robes

(Ps. 44) in order to suggest the beauty and diversity of the Church.

2. The greater fullness of life following from the variety of practice is sufficiently mentioned in the following lines, where it says expressly that this diversity 'makes no slight contribution to the fulfillment of her mission'.

The second version had said that the Churches of the East had the duty to govern themselves according to their own orders. Three Fathers objected to the word duty (*officium*). They felt that the Eastern Churches ought to be left free also to change their orders sometimes. The Secretariat for Unity pointed out that later the good of souls was mentioned; any alterations or adaptations to the demands of our times should be carried out according to their own traditions. The *modus* of the three Fathers was taken into consideration by an alteration of 19 November, 1964, changing duty to opportunity (*facultas*). This alteration emphasizes the freedom in adaptation, which should be carried out according to the special Eastern traditions. This is specially prescribed in articles 5 and 6 of the decree 'On the Catholic Eastern Churches'.

One Father proposed the following alteration for the final sentence of this article: 'The perfect restoration and observance of this principle, to be as widely embracing as it had been during the thousand years of unity with these Churches, though it had not always been observed . . . .' According to this Father this addition would also agree with article 9 of the decree 'On the Catholic Eastern Churches'. The Secretariat for Unity replied that the proposal was right in that the observance of this principle did not apply only to the present discipline of the Easterns but also to its perfect restoration, which is a condition of unity. The proposal, however, limits the application of the principle too much, because it does not take sufficient account of the demands and progress of the ecumenical movement in the present and the future.

One Father opposed the words 'it has not always been maintained' on the grounds that they were unnecessary, polemical and a kind of self-accusation betraying exaggerated humility. The Secretariat for Unity replied that the text only expresses an obvious historical fact presented in simple sincerity, without polemic or exaggeration.

Another Father wanted 'essential' in the last clause to be replaced by 'almost essential', because this was not a *condicio de iure* but a condition essential in practice. This *modus*, too, was rejected, since the distinction was scarcely intelligible.

THE SPECIAL CHARACTERISTICS OF THE EASTERNS IN TREATING DIVINE DOCTRINE

17. The principles here enunciated, with regard to legitimate diversity, hold good in the case of diversity in the theological expression of teaching. When revealed truth is explored there is a difference to be seen in the methods and approaches of the East and the West to the understanding and statement of divinity. It is not surprising that perception of revealed mystery on the one side is occasionally more penetrating than the other's, and set in a better light. Consequently it must be admitted that, in such cases, the theological expressions which differ are often complementary rather than contradictory. As far as the genuine theological traditions of Eastern Christians are concerned, they are admittedly remarkably well rooted in the sacred scriptures, they find their support and their expression in the life of the liturgy, they draw sustenance from the living traditions of the apostles and from the writings of the Eastern Fathers and spiritual writers, their tendency is towards the right ordering of life or, rather, to the full contemplation of Christian truth.

Sometimes the authentic traditions of East and West complement each other. This became clear, for example, during the discussions of the Council of Florence on the procession of the Holy Spirit. Many Eastern traditions are identical with those of the West, though slightly differently expressed.

One Father feared that this section confirmed erroneous Eastern ideas. The reply pointed out that only authentic theological traditions were referred to.

Another Father thought the text might be misunderstood so as to imply that there were no doctrinal differences between the Catholic and the Orthodox Churches. The Secretariat replied that doctrinal differences were not mentioned in this passage because, on the one hand, this was not the place for it and, on the other, because the words 'genuine traditions' sufficiently removed the danger of a misunderstanding.

Another proposal suggested that in the sentence about the different theological formulas complementing rather than contradicting each other a 'very often' should be inserted. The Secretariat for Unity considered that this was already implied in the 'rather', which meant 'not always and not in every case'. In order to make this clearer a *non raro* (literally: not rarely) was inserted on 19 November, 1964.

A further *modus* pointed out that Latin theologians, for

example St Thomas Aquinas, had indeed borrowed and integrated much that was good from Eastern theology, but that not everything in this theology was correct. Hence the two theologies could not simply be said to complement each other.

The reply again referred to the term 'genuine traditions'. It was a historical fact that Eastern and Western theologies complemented each other. Through mutual explanations and better understanding it frequently became clear that apparent contradictions actually complemented each other. The text did not refer to borrowings of Western from Eastern theologians.

One Father thought the last sentence of this paragraph exaggerated. The phrase 'towards the right ordering of life' should be left out, or at least the words 'to the full contemplation of Christian truth' should be replaced by 'to a fuller contemplation of Christian truth'.

This *modus*, too, was not accepted, for the following reasons:

1. The text corresponds to the truth and only states a fact.

2. 'Fuller' would not be a useful change, since the word 'tendency' sufficiently expresses the comparative character. It is not said that through the apostolic tradition and the writings of the Fathers Christian truth is actually fully contemplated, but only that these tend to such a contemplation. Now this is the object of all theology, especially with the Easterns.

Finally one of the Fathers wanted the words 'the living traditions of the apostles' to be left out. According to this objection the apostolic tradition is the source of divine revelation, and hence is necessarily common to East and

West. It could therefore not be mentioned among the causes of difference between the two.

The Secretariat for Unity replied:

1. The text does not say that the living tradition is among the causes for the differences between East and West. It belongs to them as little as sacred scripture, the liturgy and the writings of the Fathers which are mentioned in the text together with the apostolic tradition.

2. The apostolic tradition is the common source in the whole Church; but it nourishes the Western Christians differently from the Easterns, since each emphasize matters differently.

This sacred Synod thanks God that many Eastern children of the Catholic Church who keep guard over their inheritance and desire to live with greater freedom from fault, with greater fullness, are now living in full communion with their brethren who support the tradition of the West. It declares that the whole of this heritage, spiritual and liturgical, disciplinary and theological, in its varying traditions, is relevant to the fully catholic and apostolic character of the Church.

Those Eastern Churches that live in full ecclesial communion with the Apostolic Roman See (often called, not very suitably, Uniate Churches) are mentioned and praised because they have preserved the Eastern traditions. The present decree leaves the treatment of these Churches to the decree 'On the Eastern Catholic Churches'. In the case of both decrees it is important to realize with which Eastern Churches they are concerned.

It is of basic significance that the decree says the differences in the spiritual, liturgical, disciplinary and theological patrimony manifest not only the catholicity, but also the apostolicity of the Church. Articles 15 to 17, and indeed the whole first part of Chapter Three make it clear that the rite is more than a special liturgy, more than certain rubrics and usages that are a matter of discipline. The rite is something much deeper and can be understood only within a special ecclesiological and anthropological framework. It is difficult to define the rite in which all the traditions of a Church and its special way of life in Christ are expressed. As on similar occasions, the decree has here used a descriptive presentation. In the decree 'On the Eastern Churches' the term 'rite' is frequently used and always means the whole of liturgical, disciplinary, spiritual and theological traditions, unless it is evident from the wording of the context that only the liturgy is meant.

The constitution 'On the Sacred Liturgy' says in article 4 of its Preface that, faithful to tradition, the Church accords the same right and honour to all recognized rites which in future, too, are to be preserved and encouraged in every way.

CONCLUSION

18. *After thorough scrutiny of these points, the sacred Synod repeats the statement of past Councils and Roman pontiffs: if fellowship and unity are to be restored, 'no burden should be imposed beyond those which cannot be avoided' (Acts 15:28). It eagerly desires that, from now on, every effort be directed towards the gradual achievement of unity, in the different institutions and forms of the Church's life, chiefly by prayer and brotherly dialogue on the subjects of doctrine and the requirements of the pastoral office, to which our age gives increased urgency. In the same way, it brings to the notice of the faithful and the pastors of the Catholic*

*Church their ties of kinship with men who have left the East and
are spending their lives far from their homeland. It is hoping
thereby for an increase in brotherly co-operation with them, in a
spirit of charity from which every breath of faction and rivalry is
excluded. If this work is promoted wholeheartedly, the sacred
Synod hopes that, with the removal of the wall dividing the
Western from the Eastern Church, one single building will, at
long last, come into existence, firmly based on its corner-stone,
Christ Jesus, who will make them both one.*[1]

The principle enunciated by the Council of Apostles in
Acts 15:28 is equally valid for the Churches and ecclesial
communities separated from the Roman See in the West.
The second version had only said 'for the restoration of
communion and union'. Nine Fathers observed that the
principle stated by the Council of Apostles was necessary not
only for the restoration but also for the preservation of the
unity of the Church. Hence the restoration need not be
mentioned, it need only be said to be 'necessary for communion and union'.

The Secretariat for Unity retained the mention of
restoration because it was particularly applicable in this
decree. The suggestion of the nine Fathers was, however,
admitted to be right, hence the final text has '*restorandum vel
servandum*'.[2]

One Father wanted 'in secular matters' to be added to the
words 'brotherly dialogue'. This proposal was rejected,
because the brotherly co-operation is meant to be extended
also to the common pastoral needs of modern Christendom.

---

[1] Cf. Council of Florence, session VI (1439), Definitio *Laetentur caeli*, in
Mansi 31, 1026 a.

[2] 'To be restored and preserved'—a nuance which is lost in the C.T.S.
English translation.

In this way, too, the restoration of ecclesial communion could gradually be prepared and develop.

The formula of the Council of Florence about the removal of the wall dividing the Eastern and Western Churches is very important for the relationship of the two Churches. One of the Fathers asked what was to be understood by this wall, whether it signified only accidental differences, such as different theological expressions complementing each other? The answer was that according to the decree of the Council of Florence the wall signified everything in the way of full ecclesial communion.

II. The Separated Churches and Ecclesial Communities in the West

As has been said before, the decree does not state exactly to whom the terms Church and ecclesial community apply. Certainly, among the communities sprung from Protestantism, there are those that reject the title of 'Church', while others decidedly claim it. It is understandable that the Council did not want to go into details here, nevertheless, the decree clearly tends to emphasize the ecclesial elements of the denominations that originated from the Reformation. In the discussion of the schema this was demanded especially by those Fathers who wanted the term 'Church' applied analogously to the reformed communities also.

Indeed, there is no large Christian community that does not admit that its members owe their faith in Jesus Christ to an ecclesial mediation, however much some play down this mediation. Every Christian worthy of the name owes his connexion with Christ to faith in the redeemer and the baptism which have been mediated to him by the preaching and the administration of the sacraments of a community. Every truly Christian denomination includes some mediation that has an ecclesial structure. This was strongly emphasized by the Reformers in their fight against the Anabaptists, the enthusiasts and the 'heavenly prophets'. Though in some Christian communions the ecclesial elements may be reduced to a minimum, they are nevertheless present in all the great denominations. This is true especially of baptism, whose ecclesial importance is strongly emphasized in the decree. Faith in Jesus Christ as Son of God and redeemer in connexion with the sacramental sign of baptism creates a visible ecclesial community however much reduced it may be in certain cases. In this way there exists an elementary unity among all Christian denominations which alone makes actual ecumenism possible. Baptism effects integration into Christ, creating a rudimentary, as yet imperfect unity of Christians which is not only invisible but, by virtue of the sacramental sign of baptism, visible also. The decree mentions these matters in article 22 when dealing with the sacramental life of the Western Christians separated from us.

The Special Situation of these Communities

19. Churches and ecclesial communities were separated from the Holy See in the serious disturbances which started in the West at the close of the Middle Ages, or, some of them, at a later date. They are all connected with the Catholic Church by special family ties arising from the day to day living of the Christian life in ecclesiastical fellowship in the preceding centuries.

The diversity of origin, doctrine and spiritual life of these churches and communities makes them very different from us and from each other. It is a difficult task to classify them adequately and we have no intention of attempting it here.

Without going into a detailed explanation of the historical causes of the Reformation the Council indicates only quite generally the complicated situation of late medieval Christianity, which was an important factor in the divisions of the Church. 'The close of the Middle Ages or later' is deliberately vague so as to include post-Reformation separations such as the Old Catholic Church.

The decree does not give a description of these Churches and ecclesial communities. While the first version of the schema simply enumerated all the common elements retained by all Christians in a somewhat static manner, the second version presented them as the starting point for a dialogue which ought to be begun and continued. This method, which corresponded to the suggestions of many observer delegates, also pleased the Fathers, because in this way the differences became more evident.

The ecumenical movement and desire for peace with the Catholic Church has not yet gathered strength everywhere. Nevertheless, we are hopeful that an ecumenical sentiment will gradually grow among all, together with mutual esteem.

In the discussion several Latin-American Fathers had pointed out that the ecumenical attitude was by no means so widespread as might seem from the first draft of the schema. They called to mind the vehement polemics of certain sects against the Catholic Church. Hence this new paragraph was inserted into the second version of the schema: after the Council had asked all Catholic Christians to be ecumenically minded and to act accordingly, it now expresses the hope that the ecumenical attitude may increase among all Christians.

This declaration had not removed all difficulties. One written request on this paragraph demanded an explicit condemnation of all forms of 'proselytism' working with offers of money and other unfair means of propaganda in places where Christ had already been preached, thus creating confusion among the faithful and leading to indifferentism. The Secretariat for Unity replied with two statements:

1. The ecumenical movement itself offers a remedy against such objectionable methods of 'proselytism'. This is clear from the declaration made by the World Council of Churches at its congress at New Delhi as well as from the fact that certain sects which are most active in 'proselytizing' reject the ecumenical movement and do not participate in its work.

2. The decree 'On Ecumenism' itself cannot deal with 'proselytism'. This will be dealt with in the 'Declaration on Religious Liberty' as well as in the *Directorium Oecumenicum* which will be produced by the Secretariat for Christian Unity.

It has, however, to be admitted that there do exist serious differences between these churches and communities and the Catholic Church, differences of historical, sociological, psychological outlook and, primarily, in the interpretation of revealed truth. Our purpose is to facilitate the initiation of ecumenical dialogue despite these differences. In what follows, our wish is to publish some of the possible and essential bases and stimuli to this dialogue.

Both inside and outside the Council this part of the first

draft of the schema was accused of being too optimistic. But here the Council speaks of ecumenism realistically, gravely emphasizing both the theological and the non-theological factors of the separation in order thus to explain once more the reasons for the ecumenical dialogue.

One Father proposed to speak of 'dogmas' rather than of 'revealed truth'. Three Fathers wanted an addition on the constitution of the Church. Another Father proposed to say: 'especially concerning the integrity and interpretation of revealed truth'. For the differences did not only concern the interpretation of holy scripture but also the doctrine of tradition and the integrity of the canon.

The Secretariat for Unity did not accept these *modi*, because revealed truth is a larger concept than dogma, holy scripture or the constitution of the Church. It was not a question of explaining the scriptures but of expounding the whole of revealed truth. Revealed truth itself is one, but it is differently explained in the different Christian denominations.

The Council gives the reasons for the separation in the words 'serious differences . . . primarily in the interpretation of revealed truth', indicating at the same time that it does not mean to declare reformed Christianity to be a kind of fragmentary Catholicism. Such a quantitative view would not do justice to the special characteristics of the Reformation and misjudge the deeper causes of the separation. Titular Archbishop Émile Blanchet, the rector of the Institut Catholique in Paris, said in the Council hall: 'The reformed system is more than a number of dogmas which could be sufficiently refuted by a few good arguments. Behind these propositions lies a special view of revelation which is different from the Catholic one . . . The conception of the Reformers resulted from an exaggerated regard for certain aspects of the Christian truth, which led to the danger of overlooking or denying other aspects.' The Council was satisfied with the statement of the decree.

ON CONFESSING CHRIST

20. We envisage first the Christians who give glory to the one God, Father, Son and Holy Spirit, by publicly acknowledging Jesus Christ as God and Lord and sole mediator between God and mankind. We are aware that there do exist considerable disagreements with Catholic doctrine, even on the subject of Christ, the incarnate Word of God, and on the work of redemption, as well as the mystery and the ministry of the Church, and Mary's function in the work of salvation. It gives us joy, all the same, to observe that our separated brethren look to Christ as the source and centre of ecclesiastical fellowship. Their longing for union with Christ compels them to engage ever more deeply in the quest for unity, and also to bear witness among nations all over the world to their belief.

This paragraph again points to the basic formula of the World Council of Churches at New Delhi. The theological differences in Christology, soteriology, ecclesiology and mariology are mentioned. The Council is, however, content with a simple enumeration, leaving the discussion of the deeper causes and connexions to the theologians. In the opinion of Congar the distinctive doctrines of Catholic and Protestant Christians can be reduced to different concepts of Christology. The Council simply states that while happy that the separated brethren confess Christ they are yet well aware of the differences that have been mentioned.

One Father suggested replacing 'first' by 'only', since only those who believed that Christ is the Son of God could be called Christians. The suggestion was rejected, because the word 'first' referred to those Christians who confess their faith openly before the world.

Another Father, moved by a similar fear, proposed supplementing the second version of the schema 'Jesus Christ as Lord and sole mediator' by the addition 'as God'. The Secretariat for Unity expressed its conviction that those Christians who deny the divinity of Christ are Christians only in a very analogous sense. The proposal to insert the words 'as God' was accepted in order to emphasize that our separated brethren confess the divinity of Christ.

One Father wanted the words 'considerable disagreements' replaced by 'fundamental disagreements'. The Secretariat for Unity said in its reply that not all differences are fundamental and that the word 'considerable' includes the fundamental ones as well as the others.

Seventeen Fathers thought that the last words of article 20 expressed uncalled-for praise. The Secretariat for Unity replied that they merely stated an undeniable fact already mentioned in article 4 of the first chapter.

The Study of Holy Scripture

21. Their love, their respect, their near-worship for the sacred scriptures lead them to sustained and skilful study of the sacred pages: the gospel 'is an instrument of God's power that brings salvation to all who believe in it, Jew first and then Greek' (Rom. 1:16).

One Father objected to the word 'near-worship', because

this might appear unbiblical and offensive to Protestants. The reply pointed out that many Protestants often use this word, especially among the French-speaking peoples (*culte*).

Seven Fathers wanted to say 'many of our brethren', because the text under discussion did not apply to all Protestants; there was also a destructive Protestant exegesis. This was not accepted, because the decree was not meant to go into details. It was further said about this objection that the separated brethren did not intend to destroy the scriptures, even though their exegesis occasionally had destructive results.

Three Fathers objected to the quotation of Romans 1:16, because St Paul here did not speak of the written gospel, but of the preached 'good news'. The Secretariat for Unity replied that the text of the decree, too, did not visualize written books but the Word of God that is found in holy scripture, and the gospel which is the good news. This meaning was presupposed also in the following paragraph of article 21.

They call upon the Holy Spirit and seek God in the text of the sacred scriptures, in the conviction that he is speaking to them in Christ, who was foretold by the prophets, the Word made flesh on our behalf. In the scriptures they contemplate the life of Christ and the teachings of the divine Master, and the acts that he performed for the salvation of mankind, especially the mysteries of his death and resurrection.

In the second version of the schema this paragraph had begun: 'Impelled by the Holy Spirit they find God, who speaks to them in Christ, in holy scripture. . .'.

One Father wanted this and the following sentence left out. Three Fathers required the words 'impelled by the Holy

Spirit' to be removed. They gave as their reason that the terms of the text seemed to confirm the teaching of the Reformers, according to which every believer receives the inner light of the Holy Spirit in such a way that the teaching office of the Church is superfluous.

Another Father asked to replace 'find' by 'seek'. He did not give a reason for this, but he evidently shared the fears of the above-mentioned Fathers. The Secretariat for Unity tried to allay these fears by saying that the Holy Spirit undoubtedly works in the non-Catholic Christians and that it was not the Council's business to judge the results of this activity. The text certainly did not exclude the necessity of the Church's teaching office, which was expressly affirmed in the following sentences of this article.

It seems that the doubts of a group of Fathers were not quietened by these explanations. They were met by an alteration inserted on 19 November, 1964 which constitutes the final text. Many Fathers as well as the observer delegates felt that this was the most serious change, though its content is quite in accordance with the whole trend of the decree. Hence, on the afternoon of 19 November, one observer delegate said that while he would not have found anything unusual if the passage had been in the original, yet now that he could compare it with the earlier version, it was painful for him that 'find' had been replaced by 'seek', which was definitely a watering down.

In order rightly to judge the meaning and scope of this change the following considerations should be borne in mind:

1. In articles 3 and 4 of Chapter One the decree explicitly says that the Holy Spirit is also at work in the separated

brethren and their communities, indeed this is presupposed by the whole text. This accords with article 15 of the dogmatic constitution *De Ecclesia* which says that the Church is for several reasons related to those who are baptized, who share the honourable name of Christians but do not confess the full faith and do not preserve the unity of communion with the successor of Peter. The constitution admits that many honour the scriptures as the norm of faith and life, show a sincere religious zeal, believe lovingly in God, the Father almighty and in Christ the Son of God and redeemer, that they receive the sign of baptism which unites them to Christ and even acknowledge and receive other sacraments in their own Churches or ecclesial communities. To this must be added communion in prayer and other spiritual goods, indeed a true union in the Holy Spirit who with his gifts and graces is at work in them also with his sanctifying power and has strengthened some of them even unto the shedding of blood.

2. The alteration was due to the fear that the earlier text could be misinterpreted to mean that the pious reading of scripture would give the individual reader automatic and unerring knowledge of the truth of revelation contained in it. The change was designed to exclude subjective under-standing of the bible divorced from its ecclesiological dimension. Nevertheless, the present text does not want to weaken the fact that in the devout reading of scripture, reformed as well as other Christians know Christ as the Son of God, the Lord and redeemer, by faith through the grace of the Holy Spirit, and that they not only seek but also find him. St Augustine as well as Pascal has said that no one truly seeks God who has not already somehow found him.

At Pope Paul's reception of the observer delegates on 17 October, 1963 Professor Skydsgaard said: 'In the love of Christ truth must be sought to be found; to find it we must seek it, and once found, we must go on seeking, as St Augustine says.' The Pope replied: 'Seek in order to find, and find so as to seek still more: this phrase of St Augustine, which gave us much pleasure, Professor, to hear you quoting, concerns us all: a real Christian can never be static.'[1]

3. The *quasi* (as, viz. he speaks to them) is not to be translated 'as if', as has unfortunately sometimes been done. Classical Latin uses *quasi* in comparative clauses in the sense of 'as', and thus it is always used in later, and especially in ecclesiastical Latin. It is used in this sense in the Vulgate translation of the Prologue of St John's gospel: We have beheld his glory, glory as (*quasi*) of the only Son of the Father' (John 1:14).

Cardinal Bea has said about article 21: 'In its present form the decree in no way denies the New Testament doctrine— and could not deny it as such—that the non-Catholic brethren, as every baptized person in general, is under the guidance of the Holy Spirit; that this holds even more true in such a sacred action as the reading of the Word of God in holy scripture.

'In another place the Council clearly states that holy scripture is the inspired Word of God. Hence it is God himself who speaks to man in the reading of scripture. Hence it is absolutely wrong to translate the relevant passage of the decree, as is frequently done, "they seek God in the sacred scriptures as if he spoke to them in Christ". It must rather be

[1] The text of both these speeches is given in full in Y. Congar, *Report from Rome II*, London, 1964.

translated: "They (non-Catholic Christians) call upon the Holy Spirit and seek God in the text of the sacred scriptures, in the conviction that he is speaking to them in Christ." Thus the alteration of the text does not deny any of the truths that have been mentioned.'[1]

Incidentally the Reformers, too, condemned a subjectivist interpretation of scripture without any ecclesial relations in their controversies with the Anabaptists and other enthusiasts who claimed to be guided by the Holy Spirit alone, refusing to recognize any other authority. This point of view, however, did not influence the terminology of the present text, because the Council deliberately abstained from a 'description of the Reformation Churches'. As was done in all the other articles of this part, in the first two paragraphs of article 21 the Council wanted to point out some elements of the common Christian inheritance in order in the next section to explain the differences.

When Christians separated from us maintain the divine authority of the sacred books, they think in a different way to us—and differ among themselves—about the relation of the scriptures with the Church; for in the Church our Catholic faith asserts that the true magisterium enjoys a unique position when it comes to the exposition and preaching of the written Word of God.

Nevertheless, in the dialogue, the sacred utterances are surpassing instruments in the powerful hand of God for winning the unity which the Saviour offers to all men.

On 15 November, 1961, Cardinal Bea gave a lecture at the University of Fribourg (Switzerland) on 'How university research and teaching can further Christian unity'. He said that in the sphere of biblical scholarship, the age of

[1] In *Christ und Welt* 18 (1965) 5, p. 11.

attack and counter attack is long over, and that serious efforts are now being made to remove differences of opinion by quiet and objective discussion. He foresaw that in the ecumenical work of the Council, holy scripture would play an important part; 'for it is the common ground on which we and our separated brethren stand . . . . All who take part in the ecumenical movement or come into contact with it will need knowledge of sacred scripture. This knowledge should be wide, exact and based upon a sound, methodical analysis. It should not be confined to exegesis in the narrow sense but should include true biblical theology, which is a synthesis of detailed exegetical work. Publications dealing with problems of unity should be grounded on a real scholarly knowledge of the bible. The teaching of exegesis must be thorough but it must also take sufficient account of ecumenical questions. It is providential that Pius XII, in his encyclical *Divino Afflante Spiritu*, attached such great importance to biblical theology . . . . This requirement applies in general to the work of exegetes; but it is especially important for sound preparation of theological discussions with those of other faiths.'[1]

THE SACRAMENTAL LIFE

22. *Whenever the sacrament of baptism is duly conferred and accepted with the right disposition, it really incorporates a man in Christ who has been crucified and is now in glory. It gives him fresh birth into a partnership in the divine life, as the apostle says: 'You, by baptism, have been united with his burial, united too,*

[1] Cardinal Bea, *The Unity of Christians*, London, 1963, pp. 101-2.

with his resurrection, through your faith in that act of power by which God raised him from the dead' (Col. 2:12).[1]

Baptism, then, sets up a sacramental bond of unity existing among all those who have had rebirth through him. But, in itself, baptism is only a beginning, an introduction, for it is wholly directed to the acquisition of the fullness of life in Christ. Baptism is orientated to the complete profession of faith, the complete incorporation in the institute of salvation, as Christ wanted, the complete integration into the fellowship of the eucharist.

The question of the proper administration of baptism according to its institution by Jesus Christ is only briefly touched upon. In the discussion of the first version of the schema it had been suggested that the decree should urgently request the Protestant communities to see to it that baptism was always and everywhere administered in such a way as to leave no doubt about its validity. In support of this suggestion it was pointed out that we had cause to doubt the validity of baptism administered by Protestant clergymen in certain places. Some Fathers also wished the Protestant authorities to give a clearer exposition of their doctrine of marriage so as to facilitate new regulations for mixed marriages.

The Council, however, was of the opinion that such proposals and suggestions could not be included in the decree 'On Ecumenism'. Perhaps something might be said about these things in the *Directorium Oecumenicum* in a form acceptable to our separated brethren. The question of the valid administration of baptism could best be clarified by direct contacts in the various districts.

Ecclesial communities separated from us may be lacking the full

[1] Cf. Rom. 6:4.

unity with us which derives from baptism; we may believe them to have failed to preserve the whole, authentic substance of the mystery of the eucharist, especially in view of their lack of the sacrament of order. Nevertheless, they do enact the memorial at the Last Supper of the Lord's death and resurrection and, in so doing, they proclaim that its meaning is life in the fellowship of Christ and they are looking forward to his coming in glory. For this reason, the teaching on the Lord's Supper, the other sacraments, the worship and ministry of the Church should constitute the subject matter of the dialogue.

Discussion of the eucharist is one of the most important objects of the ecumenical dialogue; hence the Council wants briefly to indicate the main differences, without bypassing the positive elements of non-Catholic eucharistic piety.

The second version of the schema wanted to meet both these concerns by a special paragraph which in the original began with the words: 'Though the ecclesial communities ... have not preserved the full reality of the eucharist, especially because of the defect of the sacrament of order.' The statement that these communities 'have not preserved the full reality of the eucharist' met with objections from several Fathers, who expressed this by their *modi* on the vote.

Some Fathers objected to the word 'especially'. There are other reasons why these communities had not preserved 'the full reality of the eucharist', for example their different doctrine of the eucharist. It was pointed out in the reply that the word 'especially' did admit other reasons, besides the defect of the sacrament of orders.

One Father said that the statement on the lack of full reality of the eucharist was not true of all the communities discussed by this second part of Chapter Three: it did not apply to the Old Catholics for example. The Secretariat for Unity explained that the term 'especially' left room for such exceptions.

Most objections were directed to the words: 'the full reality of the eucharist'. One hundred and fifteen Fathers objected that many Protestants did not accept the real presence of Christ and the true eucharistic sacrifice. Four Fathers mentioned the Protestant doctrine of a merely dynamic presence, probably with Calvin in mind. They also referred to a merely 'logical' presence, a difficult expression which was perhaps meant to signify Zwingli's eucharistic doctrine. Thirteen Fathers thought that the basic defect was one of doctrine. One Father said that if the word 'full' was left out the statement would be more exact and also more acceptable to Protestants themselves than the vagueness of the present formula. Another Father expressed himself in similar terms: either the reality of the eucharist is there or it is not. There cannot be a half reality of the eucharist. When so many bishops failed to understand this expression, how could the people understand it? The expression would be a source of confusion.

The fact that in some countries the eucharistic reality is understood to mean only the real change of the bread into the body and the wine into the blood of the Lord, i.e. transubstantiation, makes it even more difficult to arrive at a right explanation of the term. Hence the objection of some of the bishops, according to whom either the full reality of the eucharist is possessed, or it is not: there can be no half-way house. On the other hand, the authors of the schema took reality to include transubstantiation and real presence, but to have a wider sense than this.

The Secretariat for Unity tried to remove these objections by a new version of the text: 'Generally speaking it may be said that the majority of Protestants believe in some presence of Christ in the eucharist. This is clear both from the teaching of the Reformers and from recent Protestant theology, as well as from the spiritual and liturgical life of Protestants. But they use other forms of expression than Catholic theologians. We must still greatly extend our mutual knowledge with the separated brethren of doctrine and spiritual life as has already been said in article 9. But since many Fathers find the present text difficult, it is proposed to say: "the full reality of the eucharistic mystery". The whole sentence then runs: "Though we believe that they have not preserved the full reality of the eucharistic mystery, especially because of the defect of the sacrament of orders".' The term 'mystery' is borrowed from biblical and patristic usage. It includes 'the marvellous and unique change' and the real presence, but has a wider and deeper meaning.

This new version could not quieten the fears of several Fathers either. On 19 November, the final version was arrived at: 'They have failed to preserve the whole, authentic substance of the mystery of the eucharist.' Even in classical Latin the word substance (*substantia*) signifies the essence of a thing as distinct from the qualities added to it. Thus Quintilianus says for example: 'The controversy concerns either the substance or the quality.' Similarly in his opening speech of the Council Pope John XXIII distinguished the substance of the doctrine of the deposit of faith from its expression. In the present decree the 'substance of the mystery of the eucharist' means its reality. The text of the final decree is meant to affirm that the differences indicated here concern the essence of the eucharist, not merely some additional details.

The second version of the schema had: 'For this reason, the teaching on the Lord's Supper, the worship and ministry of the Church should constitute the subject matter of the dialogue.'

One Father proposed the insertion of 'the other sacraments' after the Lord's Supper. He gave as his reason that the etymological meaning of *cultus* comprises only the 'latreutic'[1] part of the liturgy.

A mention of the other sacraments as a subject matter of the dialogue was acceptable because the chapter deals with the sacramental life. Hence the Secretariat for Unity accepted the proposal and included it in the final text, which states particularly that it does not mean to exclude other matters from the dialogue.

The wording of the decree urges the possibility of discussion on the connexion between the sacrament of order and the celebration of the eucharist. Article 22 once again lays down that the validity of the sacrament depends on the validity of the ministerial office, but the relation between minister and eucharist has not been defined any more closely. There is room for further study.

In canon 2 of the 22nd session the Council of Trent defined that, through Christ's words, 'Do this in commemoration of me', the apostles were ordained priests and received power to offer Christ's eucharistic body and blood. The apostles were consecrated to their priestly ministry without any external rite. They passed on their priestly and episcopal powers to their successors by the imposition of hands. In the

[1] i.e. belonging to divine worship. (Translator.)

15th century abbots who were not bishops were in individual cases empowered by the pope to confer holy orders, including that of the priesthood. In this connexion it must be remembered that in our own times simple priests have been authorized to administer the sacrament of confirmation; among the Orthodox, in contrast to the Western Church, this has always been the practice.

The constitution *De Ecclesia* declares most emphatically that the order of bishop confers the fullness of the sacrament of order, but makes no pronouncement about the historical facts mentioned above.

The *relatio* to article 21 of the constitution expressly says: 'The text states that only bishops can admit a new member to the episcopal college.' The Commission decided to make no pronouncement on the question of whether only a bishop can ordain priests. Consequently it gives no solution either to the *quaestio juris* or to the *quaestio facti*. Concerning orders conferred by priests, compare nos 1145 and 1290 of the new edition of Denzinger with canon 7 of the 23rd session of the Council of Trent (*Denz.*, 1777).

The decree 'On Ecumenism' presupposes the teaching of the constitution on the sacrament of order, but adds nothing to it. For this reason it will be possible to say that the expression used in article 22, 'in view of their lack of the sacrament of order', is not equivalent to 'in view of their lack of the approved rite of ordination'.

LIFE WITH CHRIST

23. *The Christian life of these brethren draws sustenance from belief in Christ: it gains support from the grace of baptism and*

from listening to the Word of God. It is made manifest in private prayer, reflection on the bible, Christian family life, the worship of the community gathered to praise God. In other respects their worship is frequently marked by notable elements of the ancient, communal liturgy.

Faith, where Christ is the object of belief, produces a harvest of praise and thanksgiving for the benefits received from God; there is, in addition, a lively sense of justice and a wholehearted love for the neighbour. This active faith produces a great number of organizations for the relief of spiritual and physical misery, for promoting the education of youth, the humanizing of social conditions, the establishment of peace on a world-wide scale.

There are many Christians who do not always agree with Catholics in their interpretation of the gospel in moral matters, nor on the solution of difficult, modern, social problems. Nevertheless, it is their wish, as it is ours, to remain attached to Christ's Word as the source of Christian virtue; they want to obey the apostolic command: 'Whatever you are about, in word and action alike, invoke always the name of the Lord Jesus Christ, offering your thanks to God the Father through him' (Col. 3:17). The ecumenical dialogue thus can make the moral application of the gospel its starting-point.

Some Fathers thought this text too optimistic. One Father observed that, if Protestants were so honourable and rich in virtues in some countries, this could not be said of all Protestants everywhere. Twelve Fathers proposed to add 'in many' to 'from belief in Christ' so as to avoid a generalization admitting of no exceptions. The present text was far too general in its praise.

The Secretariat for Unity replied that the text did not simply say the Protestants were honourable and virtuous;

for this could not be simply said of Catholics either. But no one ought to be considered bad if this was not clearly proved, and what was good should not be passed over in silence because of bad people. The text of the decree was not mere praise, but mentioned the true results produced by the act of faith. This was said quite generally and did not refer to individuals.

One Father proposed to remove the words 'as it is ours' in the sentence 'Nevertheless, it is their wish, as it is ours to remain attached to Christ's Word'. For if this were to be understood as referring to the objective order it seemed to presuppose that there are no doctrinal differences between Catholics and Protestants. The Secretariat for Unity replied that the text here referred to the will to adhere to the Word of Christ, not to different interpretations of this Word.

The decree mentions differences in the sphere of ethics and social teaching, some of which are very deep and must not be overlooked in the ecumenical dialogue. A German Evangelical leader, Hans Hermann Walz, speaking in 1963, dealt with these differences in his remarkable lecture on the subject 'Believers are Debtors'. He said: 'The attitude of the Church and of Christians to the world and in the world, that is to the state, society and culture—is of far more practical importance for most Protestants and Catholics, and even more for non-Christians, than direct doctrinal differences between the denominations. Attitudes to the state, Christian action in society and relations with those who do not share one's faith—these are of immediate interest. Hence this is where the prejudices concentrate, and also where new ways of common endeavour open up. Finally, in these spheres there are grave differences which we cannot overcome and which must be openly discussed.'[1]

In many cases where the gospel does not give concrete answers Catholic moralists fall back on the principles of the natural law. Evangelical ethics are determined by the doctrine of justification by faith alone and the rejection of the meritoriousness of good works resulting from it. The question of law and gospel is of central importance; it was answered differently by Luther and Calvin. In the ecumenical dialogue the discussion often focuses on whether or not the morality of the New Testament allows us to include or at least to fall back on the natural moral law.

Conclusion

24. After this brief exposition of the terms on which ecumenical action may be taken, and the principles which must control it, we turn our eyes in faith towards the future. The sacred Synod urges the faithful to refrain from any carelessness or excess of zeal, both can be damaging to the real advance of unity. Their ecumenical action can only be fully and whole-heartedly Catholic, loyal to the truth which we have had from the apostles and the Fathers; it must be in agreement too with the faith which the Catholic Church has always professed and at the same time it must aim at the fullness with which the Lord wants his body to grow with the passage of the ages.

It is the immediate hope of the sacred Synod that the initiatives of the children of the Church will keep pace with those of the

---

[1] 'Mit Konflikten leben', Kreuz-Verlag, Stuttgart-Berlin 1963, pp. 169-171. The Catholic point of view was represented by Bernhard Hanssler, ibid. 163-7.

separated brethren, that no obstacle may be set in the way of Providence and no prejudice be formed against the impulses of the Holy Spirit yet to come. It proclaims itself aware that this holy undertaking—the reconciliation of all Christians in the unity of Christ's one, single Church—is beyond human powers and human endowments. It bases its hopes on deep foundations in the prayer of Christ for the Church, in the love the Father has for us, in the power of the Holy Spirit. 'Nor does this hope delude us: the love of God has been poured out in our hearts by the Holy Spirit, whom we have received' (Rom. 5:5).

This article is the conclusion of the whole decree. Latin-American Council Fathers made many remarks and suggestions concerning the exhortation to refrain from all levity and imprudent zeal. They pointed out that a clear exposition of Catholic doctrine is especially necessary in those parts of the world where active 'proselytism' uses dishonest means and is violently opposed to the doctrine, organization and life of the Church. The Latin-American bishops were certainly in favour of ecumenism, but they wanted their special problems to be considered. They expected that the *Directorium Oecumenicum* would furnish criteria and principles for the pastoral attitude to the sects.

The Secretariat for Unity replied to this *modus*:

1. The decree had already stated that clear exposition of Catholic doctrine is necessary, in Chapter Two, article 11, as well as in this very article 24 which speaks of loyalty to the truth.

2. The ecumenical movement strengthens the struggle against these 'sects' by furthering the interior renewal of the Church.

3. The declaration 'On Religious Liberty' will contain a warning to exclude 'proselytism'.

4. Later on, the bishops' conferences will have to adapt the *Directorium Oecumenicum* of the Secretariat for Unity to the special conditions of their countries.

5. As has been said above on article 19 the whole ecumenical movement opposes the uncalled-for methods of 'proselytism' that are applied by certain sects and which are rejected by this movement.

Four factors in particular are emphasized in the final paragraph of the decree:

1. The ecumenical action of Catholics can be carried out only in full harmony with Catholic and apostolic tradition and in close relation to the faith of the Church which tends to an ever more perfect manifestation of its unity and holiness, its catholicity and apostolicity. This has once more been emphasized by Pope Paul VI in his address on 'Catholics and the Unity of the Church' of 20 January, 1965.

2. The ecumenical action of Catholic Christians is to be carried on in union with that of the Christian brethren separated from us. This emphasizes once more that the Council does not want a separate Catholic ecumenism, but that Catholics are to participate in the ecumenical movement according to the principles explained in the decree.

3. The Council declares that ecumenism is not to be bound by the decree so as to place obstacles before the new ways of Providence and the future impulses of the Holy Spirit. Thus the decree corresponds to a special historical situation of the pilgrim people of God and will leave all ways open for new ecumenical possibilities of the Church and of Christendom in the future.

4. The fulfilment of the wish for the unity of all Christians so far surpasses all human powers and faculties that it depends solely on the grace of God.

For this reason Pope Paul VI said in the general audience of 20 January, 1965: 'Anyone who is only superficially acquainted with the problem of the reunion of all Christians imagines that it can be solved quite easily and quickly. But if the historical, psychological and doctrinal data of this question are really known it becomes evident that there are on all sides great and manifold difficulties of every kind. These are so great that some despair that they can be overcome; others do not give up hope, but understand that we may need a great deal of time and certainly an intervention of God's grace that will appear to be miraculous.'[1]

For this reason the Council places all its hope in the constant prayer of Christ for his Church, in the Father's infinite love for us and in the power of the Holy Spirit, which dwells in us and has poured God's love into our hearts.

SOLEMN CONCLUSION

The Fathers have resolved on each and every utterance in this Decree. In virtue of the Apostolic power handed on to Us from Christ, We join the Venerable Fathers, in the Holy Spirit, in giving these utterances approval, decreeing them and enacting them. We order that the Synod's enactments be promulgated to the glory of God.

St Peter's, Rome, 21 November 1964.

PAUL, Bishop of the Catholic Church

The signatures of the Fathers follow.

[1] *Osservatore Romano* of 21 January, 1965, p. 1.

Part Three

The Essential Unity of the Decree
'On Ecumenism' and the Dogmatic
Constitution 'On the Church'

1. Chapter One: The Mystery of the Church

IN THE solemn final session of the Council Pope Paul VI declared that the constitution *De Ecclesia* was concerned with the central theme of the whole Council and was closely related to the decree 'On Ecumenism'.

To some extent the constitution is that sudden bursting forth of spring which John XXIII spoke of before the opening of the Council. It contains some of the finest work done during the first three sessions and, as Georges Dejaifve says, marks the Church's transition from the age of the Counter-Reformation to the ecumenical era. The constitution lays the doctrinal basis for the Church's renewal, especially if it is interpreted, as Paul VI expressly urged, in the light of its close relation to the decree 'On Ecumenism'.

The first chapter of the constitution describes the Church as a mystery—the realization of the eternal decree of the Father, the redemptive work of the Son, and the community of the Holy Spirit. This shows not only the Church's relation to the creation and her significance in the universe as a whole, but also her relation to the Most Holy Trinity, in which her pneumatological aspect is brought to the fore. Article 4 concludes this exposition by linking it with Cyprian, Augustine and John of Damascus, in the words: 'In this way the universal Church is clearly a people made one with the unity of the Father and the Son and the Holy Spirit.'

The decree 'On Ecumenism' sees in the Trinity the ultimate foundation of the unity and uniqueness of the Church, and concludes by saying: 'This is the sacred mystery of the Church's unity. The unity is established in Christ and through Christ, while the variety of gifts is the work of the Holy Spirit. The mystery has its supreme model and archetype in the unity of the Persons in the Trinity, the unity of the one God, Father and Son in the Holy Spirit' (article 2).

The constitution then describes the Church by means of the various images used in the New Testament as a gradual revelation of the mystery. In the schema submitted to the second session of the Council nothing was said about her relation to the kingdom of God, the central theme of Christ's teaching. Several of the Fathers pointed out during the discussion that the Church should be presented eschatologically as the preliminary phase of the kingdom of God. The final version of the text took these suggestions into account. After speaking of Christ's sacrifice on the cross, his eternal priesthood and his sending of the Holy Spirit, it continues:

Since then, the Church, with the equipment of her founder's gifts, in loyal observance of the charity, humility and self-denial which he commanded, accepts her mission to proclaim the kingdom of Christ and to establish it among all nations, and she sets on earth the initial shoot of this kingdom's growth. In the meantime, as she grows gradually, she sighs for the kingdom's full achievement; she hopes and longs, with all her strength, to join her King in glory (article 5).

This aspect of the Church as a pilgrim moving towards

her eschatological fulfilment appears clearly from the subsequent images drawn from the New Testament. This essential characteristic of the Church is repeatedly stressed in the schema 'On Ecumenism' and is a distinguishing feature of ecumenical ecclesiology.

The constitution's description of the Church as the bride of Christ serves also to emphasize the distinction between the Church and Christ; this distinction is often obscured in many works which treat of the Church as a continuation of Christ's life on earth. The identity of Christ with his Church has been presented in such a way as to make it seem almost an ecclesiological 'Monophysitism', as though the Church were simply a continuation of the incarnation in time and space.

After referring to the incarnation of the Word in the womb of the Virgin Mary the constitution says:

This is the divine mystery of salvation which is revealed to us and continued in the Church which the Lord set up as his own body (article 52).

In article 8, however, this analogy is more closely defined. Since the Church is a single, complex reality which is the compound of a human and a divine element:

By a significant analogy she is likened to the mystery of the Word incarnate: the nature taken by the divine Word serves as the organ of salvation, in a union with him which is indissoluble; in the same way, the social framework of the Church serves the spirit of Christ, her life-giver, for his bodily growth (cf. Eph. 4:16). The Holy Spirit, who uses the social structure of the Church for the growth of the mystical Body, is 'one and the same in the head and in the organs. It is he that gives life, unity and motion to the whole body', and so it is possible 'to compare his work to the function which is fulfilled in the human frame by the principle of life, or the soul' (article 7).

This cautious formulation stresses the pneumatological aspect, and at the same time emphasizes that the Holy Spirit is the Spirit of Christ continuing Christ's mission and building up his mystical Body. The Church is not simply the continuation of the incarnation of the Word, nor is she an incarnation of the Holy Spirit.

The constitution brings out the distinction between Christ as Head and the Church as his Body, between the incarnate Son of God as bridegroom and the Church as his bride: the Church is made up of men who have been called to justification through baptism, who are always threatened by weakness and sin, and who often fall short. For this reason the Church must continually renew herself through repentance and conversion of the heart, although she is holy through the Holy Spirit who is the invisible principle of her unity and who imparts to her Christ's gifts of grace. Thus the Church does not seek her own glory but serves her Lord in poverty of spirit and humility while waiting for his second coming.

The first chapter of the decree 'On Ecumenism' puts forward this view and the second draws conclusions from this for the 'Church called to continual reformation'. While any sort of ecclesiological 'Monophysitism' would restrict the activity and importance of the Holy Spirit, the pneumatological aspect of the Church is strongly brought out both in the constitution and in the decree.

The schema De Ecclesia, submitted at the second session on 22 April, 1963, stated plainly and without any qualification that the Church as a visible society is identical with the mystical Body of Christ: 'The visible society and the mystical Body of Christ are not two things, but one only, the compound of a human and a divine element.' On 3 October, 1963 Cardinal Lercaro, Archbishop of Bologna, made a very important intervention. He asserted that the visible Church and the mystical Body were certainly identical, but not in the same formal respect (*non secundum eandem rationem*). Church and mystical Body are in fact two separate aspects: although in the order of being established by Christ they refer to one and the same reality, in the existential, historical order they are not completely identical but exist side by side and manifest certain tensions. These tensions will persist until the end of historical time when the full identicality of Church and mystical Body will be revealed.

The cardinal proposed to qualify this statement on the identity of Church and mystical Body by saying that both formed a single reality which must be considered under two distinct aspects. In his book on the second session entitled *Coraggio del Concilio* (Brescia, 1964, p. 41), Raniero La Valle attempts to illustrate the cardinal's thought more explicitly by saying: 'The Church and the mystical Body are one and the same, but the Church as a visible society is co-extensive only with its historical dimension while the mystical Body is co-extensive with the workings of Christ's grace, and this is part of the mystery.'

Cardinal Lercaro's intervention was supported by many of the Fathers and was accorded recognition in the final text, which runs:

She is a society equipped with hierarchical organs, the mystical Body of Christ, an assembly to command attention, a spiritual fellowship. For all her richness of earthly and heavenly wealth, we must not think of the Church as two substances, but a single, complex reality, the compound of a human and a divine element (article 8).

This allows the mystical Body a 'range' extending beyond the limits of the visible Church. Article 15 of the decree goes on to declare that non-Catholic Christians are made members of the crucified and glorified Christ by baptism.

Cardinal Lercaro's first proposal is closely connected with his second. Article 8 of the schema of 22 April, 1963 had read: 'Strictly and simply speaking incorporation in the society of the Church belongs only to those who acknowledge her order in its entirety with all her established means to salvation and are united to Christ, who rules her by the agency of the Supreme Pontiff and the bishops, within her visible framework. The bonds of their union are the profession of faith, the sacraments, ecclesiastical government and fellowship.'

The cardinal proposed that the words 'strictly and simply' should be replaced by 'fully and perfectly', as had already been suggested by Bishop Carli of Segni. According to Lercaro this would mean that all baptized persons would be truly incorporated in the Church permanently and irrevocably, but that baptism alone was insufficient for a full and perfect sharing in the blessing and privileges of the Church. The proposed alteration to the text, he said, would be of ecumenical importance and was fully borne out by the Church's tradition, as many documents would prove.

This proposal, too, found its place in the final text. Article 14 of the constitution reads:

Full incorporation in the society of the Church belongs to those who are in possession of the Holy Spirit, accept her order in its entirety with all her established means to salvation, and are united to Christ, who rules her by the agency of the Supreme Pontiff and the bishops, within her visible framework. The bonds of their union are the profession of faith, the sacraments, ecclesiastical government and fellowship.

It has been the constant belief of the Catholic faith that the Church of Christ is not an entity as a hidden background to the different churches and ecclesiastical communities, and actualizing itself in these various communities. The concrete form in which the one and only Church of Christ exists is the visible Catholic Church, as article 2 of the decree declares. For this reason article 8 of the constitution says:

This Church, founded and organized in this world as a society, has its existence in the Catholic Church under the government of Peter's successor and the bishops in communion with him,[1] although outside her framework there are found many elements of holiness and truth, and they give an impetus to universal unity, in as much as they are gifts which belong to Christ's Church.

It had originally read: 'This Church, founded in this world as a society, is the Catholic Church.' The change from 'is the Catholic Church' to 'has its existence in the Catholic Church' is significant. The Latin word used means roughly 'to be there', 'to be present', 'to exist concretely'. The decree uses the same expression in article 4: '. . . the unity of the one and only Church . . . We believe that it is still in existence in the Catholic Church. . . . The word used makes allowance for the fact that there are genuine ecclesial elements in the

---

[1] She is called 'The Holy (catholic apostolic) Roman Church': *Prof. fidei Trid.*, loc. cit. and Vatican Council I Sess. III, Const. dogm. *de fide cath.*: Denz. 1782 (3001).

separated churches and ecclesiastical communities. The *relatio* says: 'The word *subsistit* (has its existence in) is used so that the whole statement may be more in accordance with the affirmation of the ecclesial elements which are to be found elsewhere'.

In article 8 of the same *relatio*, the theological commission gave the reasons behind the emendations to article 8 of the constitution:

A description was given of the hidden spiritual means by which the Church is joined for all time to Christ. The intention was to show that this Church here on earth is concretely to be found in the Catholic Church. This empirical Church manifests Christ's mystery, albeit in darkness, until the time when it shall be made manifest in the fullness of light. Thus Christ himself endured humiliation before entering into his glory. In this way it will be possible to avoid any impression that the description of the Church offered by the Council is purely unreal and idealistic. For the sake of clearer understanding the matter was subdivided and the following points dealt with in order:

(*a*) The mystery of the Church is present and manifests itself in a concrete society. But the visible society and the spiritual element are not two things but *one* complex reality embracing the divine and human, the means of salvation and also the fruits of salvation. This is illustrated by a comparison with the Word made flesh.

(*b*) The Church is one and unique and she subsists here on earth in the Catholic Church, even though ecclesial elements are to be found outside the Catholic Church.

(c) The manifestation of the mystery of the Catholic Church is made at one and the same time in strength and in weakness, even in the circumstances of poverty, persecution, sin and purification, so that the Church may become like Christ, though he was without sin. The theme of poverty was discussed more thoroughly than some of the Fathers would have wished.

(d) But the Church overcomes these difficulties through the power of Christ, and through love, through which it reveals his mystery—albeit in darkness—until the time when it shall be made manifest in the fullness of light.

The *relatio generalis* on the first chapter of the constitution says: 'The mystery of the Church is not an unreal or idealistic image but exists in the concrete Catholic society under the guidance of the successor of Peter and of the bishops in his *communio*. There are not two Churches, but only one, which is both of heaven and of earth, and which manifests God's eternal decree by becoming like her Lord both in his humiliation and in his glorious victory.'

The decree 'On Ecumenism' presupposes this concept of the Church and comments on it specifically from the ecumenical aspect in the first chapter, which deals not only with the unity and uniqueness of the Church but also with the part played by the separated communities in the work of salvation; the second chapter draws practical conclusions, and the third considers the ecclesial elements in the separated communities and in particular their relation to the Catholic Church.

2. Chapter Two: The People of God

THIS chapter was originally a part of the third chapter *De laicis* and followed after the chapter *De constitutione hierarchica Ecclesiae*. As a result of a suggestion by Cardinal Suenens the co-ordinating commission decided to treat the people of God separately in the second chapter. It proved to be an extremely happy solution. In this way the Church as a whole appears as the bearer of the means of salvation, as the community of life, love and truth established by Christ, as the instrument of redemption, as the light of the world, and as the people of God on pilgrimage towards its eschatological fulfilment. In his commentary on Ephesians, cap. IV, lect. 2, Thomas Aquinas depicts the unity of the Church and uses the image of the City of God, whose Head is Christ crucified and glorified, whose law, as the *lex fidei*, excludes all self-satisfaction, whose signs are baptism and the other sacraments, whose ultimate goal is the kingdom of glory which Christ will hand over to the Father, and whose majesty is received from the divine power of the Father, the wisdom of the Son and the grace of the Holy Spirit.

In a similar way article 9 of the constitution says:

This messianic people has for its head Christ 'who was handed over to death for our sins, and raised to life for our justification' (Rom. 4:25); now he is in possession of the name which is greater than any other name and reigning in glory in heaven. For rank it has the dignity and freedom of God's sons, whose hearts are like a temple, the dwelling-place of the Holy Spirit. For law it has the new commandment of a love like the love Christ has shown us (cf. John 13:34). For goal it has the kingdom of God; it has had its beginning at the hands of God himself on earth, it must be spread further until it shall have its consummation from him at the end of the ages, when Christ, our life, has appeared (cf. Col. 3:4) and 'nature in its turn will be set free from the tyranny of corruption to share in the glorious freedom of God's sons' (Rom. 8:21).

While Thomas Aquinas tends to describe the unity of the *Civitas Dei* in a static way, the Council emphasizes more strongly the dynamic aspect of the one people of God on the way to its eschatological fulfilment:

Israel according to nature, on pilgrimage in the desert, already had the name of God's 'Church' (2 Esds. 13:1; cf. Num. 20:4; Deut. 23:1 ff.). Just so, the new Israel, making its way through the present age and in search of the city that is to come (cf. Heb. 13:14), is also called the 'Church of Christ' (cf. Matt. 16:18). Christ it was who won it for himself at the price of his own blood (cf. Acts 20:28), who filled it with his spirit and fitted it out with the appropriate means to the visible union of a society. God has convened the assembly of those who fix their eyes, in belief, on Jesus, the author of salvation, the principle of unity and peace, and he has erected the Church to be, for each and all, the visible sacrament of this saving unity.[1] She is to extend to all lands; she enters human history, yet she transcends the ages and the boundaries of nations. On her progress through temptations and troubles the strength of God's grace that the Lord promised her, gives her the courage not to fall away from perfect loyalty, through weakness of

---

[1] Cf. St Cyprian, *Epist.* 69, 6: PL 3, 1142 B; Hartel, 3 B, p. 754: 'The inseparable sacrament of unity'.

nature, but to persist as a bride worthy of her Lord, to renew herself by the activity of the Holy Spirit without intermission, until, by way of the cross, she reaches the light, which knows no nightfall.

The detailed discussion of the priestly, prophetic and kingly character of the people of God, which includes not only all nations and races but also the various ministerial grades of the Church, leads into an account of the grades of incorporation into the Church, 'which men enter by the gateway of baptism'. Article 15 explains the connexion of non-Catholic Christians with the Church:

The Church has come to recognize several reasons for her connexion with those who are baptized and have the honour of the name of Christian, yet do not profess the faith in its entirety, or maintain union in fellowship under Peter's successor.[1] There are a great number who honour the sacred scripture as the norm of belief and life and who show sincere religious zeal. They have a loving faith in God the Father almighty and in Christ, his Son, our Saviour.[2] They are marked by baptism and thereby joined to Christ; they acknowledge other sacraments too and receive them in their own churches or ecclesiastical communities. Several of them possess the episcopate, celebrate the holy eucharist and encourage piety towards the Virgin Mother of God.[3] They also have a fellowship in prayer and in other spiritual benefits, and a real union in the Holy Spirit, for he is at work among them too with his power of sanctification in gifts and graces: he has given some

[1] Cf. Leo XIII, Apost. Letter *Praeclara gratulationis*, 20 June 1894: ASS 26 (1893-4) p. 707.

[2] Cf. Leo XIII, Encycl. *Satis cognitum*, 29 June 1896: AAS 28 (1895-6) p. 738. Encycl. *Caritatis studium*, 25 July 1898: AAS 31 (1898-9) p. 11. Pius XII, Broadcast *Nell'alba*, 24 Dec. 1941: AAS 34 (1942) p. 21.

[3] Cf. Pius XI, Encycl. *Rerum Orientalium*, 8 Sept. 1928: AAS 20 (1928) p. 287, Pius XII, Encycl. *Orientalis Ecclesiae*, 9 April 1944: AAS 36 (1944) p. 137.

of them strength to the extent of shedding their blood. So it is that the Spirit is rousing in all Christ's disciples desire and action, in the hope that all men may be united peacefully, in the manner that Christ appointed, in one flock under one pastor.[1] *To obtain this union, Mother Church is incessantly praying, hoping and taking action, and she is exhorting her children to purification and renewal, so that the mark of Christ may shine more clearly on the face of the Church.*

The ecumenical intention of this article is clear for all to see. The constitution aims to deal with communities as well as with individuals. For this reason the words 'in their own churches or ecclesiastical communities' have been inserted in the final text. For this reason, too, the ecumenical movement is referred to: it is presented as the work of the Holy Spirit and its aims are depicted in a way reminiscent of the prayer formula of Abbé Couturier.

The *relatio* on article 15 of the constitution gives a reason for the expression 'Church and ecclesiastical communities' by declaring that the ecclesial elements enumerated here apply not only to separated Christians as individuals but also to their communities. It declares, too, that the principle underlying the whole ecumenical movement is based on this fact.

The Fathers of the Council were aware that they were here touching on the very foundations of the decree 'On Ecumenism'. A wish was expressed that the terminology of the decree should be used also for the constitution. Article 15 of the constitution, for instance, declares: 'They also have . . . a real union in the Holy Spirit, for he is at work among them too with his power of sanctification in gifts and graces.' But in the same connexion article 3 of the

[1] Cf. Instr. of Holy Office, 20 December, 1949: AAS 42 (1950) p. 142.

decree says: 'Many too of the sacred actions of the Christian religion are performed among our separated brethren. There is no doubt that they are capable of giving real birth to the life of grace.' For this reason it was suggested the terminology used in the decree should be adopted in the constitution.

The theological commission replied that both statements were in harmony with one another, since the Holy Spirit worked through the sacred actions. The commission might have added that the decree, too, in many places drew special attention to the working of the Holy Spirit in the separated communities.

3. Chapter Three: The Hierarchical Constitution of the Church and the Episcopate in Particular

CHAPTER Three continues the teaching of Vatican I on the hierarchical structure of the Church and completes it with the teaching of the apostolic college of bishops with Peter's successor as its head. During the Council's discussion on the collegiality of the bishops there was never any thought of making a separation between pope and bishops, much less of setting up an opposition between them. There is no college of bishops without their head, just as there is no apostolic college without Peter. Nor was there any thought of replacing the 'monarchical' concept of the Church with a 'parliamentary' one; the aim, rather, was to give a true account of the multiplicity of individual churches in the communion of the Church as a whole, with the Holy Spirit as the invisible principle of unity and the successor of Peter as the visible principle. It was the fundamental importance of the eucharist for the building up of the Church which threw the clearest light on this conception; the significance of this for unity is made plain in articles 4 and 15 of the decree 'On Ecumenism'.

Of special ecumenical importance is article 24 of the constitution, which says:

The mission of bishops can come into being canonically by law-ful custom, which the supreme, universal power of the Church has not revoked, by laws enacted or recognized by the same authority, or directly by the personal action of Peter's successor: but should he deny or refuse communion with the apostolic see, bishops cannot be admitted to office.[1]

In the Western Church, as a rule, jurisdiction is formally conferred by the pope. But this is not essential in all places and under all circumstances. Jurisdiction may also be conferred through legitimate right of custom which has not been specifically revoked, or through some other sort of ecclesiastical privilege. Such was the case in the first centuries of Christianity, and still is even today in the Catholic Eastern Churches, as is expressly stated in article 9 of the decree concerning these churches. This helps provide a solution to the difficult problems of the jurisdiction of Eastern bishops who are not in full communion with the Apostolic Roman See. The preliminary note of explanation to the constitution remarks on this point:

Without hierarchical communion the 'ontologico-sacramental' function (and this must be distinguished from its 'juridico-canonical' aspect) cannot be discharged. It was the decision of the commission not to enter into questions of legality and validity. They are left to theologians to discuss, specifically as far as concerns the power exercised de facto among separated Eastern Christians; there are various opinions in existence as to how this is explained.

The theological commission's reply to the 153rd *modus* to

---

[1] Cf. Code of Canon Law for the Oriental Church, c. 216-314: on patriarchs; c. 324-39: on greater archbishops; c. 362-91: on other dignitaries; in general, c. 238 §3; 216; 240; 251; 255: on the nomination of bishops by the patriarch.

the third chapter, in connexion with the text of article 24 quoted above, states: 'The separated Eastern Churches are not treated directly. In their case, recourse could be had either to the non-revocation (*non-revocatio*) of an ancient practice or to some other theological explanation.'

In article 26 of the constitution the central importance of the celebration of the eucharist is explained:

The bishop, distinguished by the fullness of the sacrament of order, is 'the steward of the grace of the high priesthood'.[1] This is particularly the case with the eucharist, which he offers himself, or whose offering is his concern;[2] and the eucharist is the direct source of life and growth for the Church. This Church of Christ is truly present in all lawful, local congregations of the faithful. These congregations, in attachment to their pastors, themselves have the names of churches in the New Testament.[3] They are, for their own locality, the new people called by God, in the Holy Spirit and in great fullness (cf. 1 Thess. 1:5). In these churches the faithful are gathered together by the preaching of Christ's gospel; in them, the mystery of the Lord's Supper is celebrated 'so that the whole brotherhood is linked by the flesh and blood of the Lord's body'.[4] Any fellowship of the altar, under the ministry of the bishop,[5] is the setting in which the symbol is shown of that charity and 'that unity of the mystical Body, without which salvation is impossible'.[6] Christ is present in these communities, though they are often small in number and resources, or widely dispersed, and by his power,

---

[1] Prayer of episcopal consecration in the Byzantine rite: *Euchologion to mega*, Rome, 1873, p. 139.

[2] Cf. St Ignatius, Martyr, *Smyrn.* 8, 1: ed. Funk, I, p. 282.

[3] Cf. Acts 8:1; 14:22-3; 20:17 and *passim*.

[4] Mozarabic prayer: PL 96, 759 B.

[5] Cf. St Ignatius, Martyr, *Smyrn.* 8, 1: ed. Funk, I p. 282.

[6] St Thomas, *Summa Theol.*, III, q. 73, a. 3.

the one, holy, catholic and apostolic Church is drawn together;[1]
*for 'the precise effect of the sharing of Christ's body and blood, is
that we pass over into what we are taking.'*[2]

Article 2 of the decree discusses the importance of the
eucharist for the unity of the Church, and article 4 says that
the aim of all ecumenical endeavours is the common celebration of the eucharist by all Christians in the unity of the
one and unique Church. It then draws an important
ecumenical conclusion in article 15: in the Eastern Churches
separated from Rome 'the celebration of the Lord's eucharist
in the individual churches builds up the Church of God and
makes it grow...'

The close connexion between the Church as mystical
Body with the Body of Christ in the eucharist was mentioned
as early as the first chapter of the constitution: the Church
builds herself up through the celebration of the eucharist
which brings men into the mystical Body of Christ and thus
gathers them together in the Holy Spirit (articles 5 and 7).
From this it is clear that the basic shape of the Church is
the liturgical assembly. The Church as a whole consists of
a communion of liturgical communities with the individual
bishops at their head.

[1] Cf. St Augustine, *C. Faustum*, 12, 20: PL 42, 265; *Serm.* 57, 7: PL 38,
389 etc.   [2] St Leo, Martyr, *Serm.* 63, 7: PL 54, 357 C.

4. Chapter Four: The Laity

THIS was the first time a Council had ever submitted a document specifically on the lay state as an *ordo* within the Church. Lay people are incorporated into Christ through baptism, share in his priestly, prophetic and kingly office, and according to their individual capacities carry out the mission of all Christian people in the world.

The job of the laity, which springs from their own vocation, is to seek the kingdom of God in the transaction of worldly business and the godly arrangement they give it. Their life is lived in the world. It is lived in each and all of the world's occupations and employments and in the ordinary situations of the life of the family and society. This is the context of their existence. This is where they have their call from God to make their contribution to the sanctification of the world from the inside, as a leaven, by tackling their own job with the same spirit of the gospel as their guide. This is the principal way in which Christ is to be shown to others, by their life's witness, in the glow of their faith, their hope and their charity. It is their especial concern to bring such light and order to the worldly business, in which they are deeply involved, that it may be performed and developed in Christ's way, and may give glory to the creator and the redeemer (article 31).

The co-operation with separated Christians recommended in article 12 of the decree is in most fields primarily a matter for the laity, who possess the particular qualifications for this and who as Christians among other Christians endeavour to order the things of this world in the light of the gospel.

Article 36 of the constitution says:

It is a great promise that is given to the disciples, a great commandment: 'Everything is for you, and you are for Christ, and Christ is for God' (1 Cor. 3:23).

There is an obligation on the faithful to recognize the inner nature of the whole of creation, its value, its orientation to the praise of God. They must help each other to greater holiness of life even by means of their secular occupations. The result to be achieved is the drenching of the world in the spirit of Christ, the surer attainment of its goal through justice, charity and peace. The chief position in the wholesale fulfilment of this duty is held by the laity. Their competence in the secular sphere and their activity have been raised intrinsically by grace to a higher level. By these means they must make vigorous efforts to see that the resources of human labour, technology, civilization, are deployed in accordance with the creator's plan and the light shed by his Word. In this case all men without exception will benefit from the cultivation of the goods of creation, these things will be more suitably distributed and will make their own contribution to universal progress in human and Christian freedom. In this way Christ will use the members of the Church to increase the shining of his saving light over the whole of human society.

The Council was well aware that any collaboration between Catholic and non-Catholic Christians, even in the social, cultural and artistic spheres would raise special problems about the way the gospel should be applied in questions of ethics and social teaching; these are spoken of in article 23 of the decree.

Article 22 of the decree calls for a dialogue with Protestants

on the ministry of the Church, which will include a discussion of the relation of the hierarchy to the laity. About
this relation the constitution says:

*A certain number are appointed by Christ's will as teachers,
stewards of God's mysteries and pastors for the sake of the others,
yet all are on a truly equal footing when it comes to the dignity and
action common to all the faithful with regard to the building of
Christ's Body. The very distinction the Lord has made between the
sacred ministers and the rest of God's people, involves a connexion,
since pastors and the rest of the faithful are tied together by their
common obligation: the Church's pastors must follow the example
of the Lord and render service to each other and to the rest of the
faithful; the faithful have to be ready to offer their associated effort
to the pastors and teachers. All in this way bear witness in their
variety to their remarkable unity in the Body of Christ. The very
diversity of graces, of services, of manifestations of power, makes a
single body of the sons of God, for 'all this is the work of one and
the same Spirit' (1 Cor. 12:11).*

*As a result of God's goodness, the laity have Christ for their
brother: for, though he is Lord of all, he did not come to have
service done to him, but to serve (cf. Matt. 20:28). Just so, they have
for brothers too the men who are appointed to the sacred ministry,
the men who exercise such pastoral care that the new commandment of charity is carried out by all; this they do by teaching,
sanctifying, governing the household of God with Christ's authorization. St Augustine has a splendid comment on this relationship:
'If my belonging to you frightens me, my being with you brings
consolation. I belong to you as bishop, I am with you as a Christian.
The first title represents a duty, the second a favour; the first
represents a risk, the second salvation'*[1] (article 32).

[1] St Augustine, *Serm.* 340, 1: PL 38, 1483.

5. Chapter Five: The Universal Vocation to Holiness in the Church

JUST as all Christians through baptism receive the same dignity, so they are all called to holiness, which consists in the perfect love of God and their neighbour.

The Lord Jesus is the divine master and exemplar of all perfection. It is he who initiates and he who puts the finishing touches to holiness of life. He preached it to each and all of his disciples, no matter what their rank: 'But you are to be perfect as your heavenly Father is perfect' (Matt. 5:48).[1] *He sent them all the Holy Spirit to stir them from within to love God with the love of their whole heart, their whole soul, their whole mind, and their whole strength (cf. Mark. 12:30) and to love each other as Christ has loved them (cf. John 13:34; 15:12). The followers of Christ have received their vocation from God not for their achievements but in accordance with his plan and his grace; they have been justified in the Lord Jesus; in the baptism of faith they have been made sons of God and partakers of the divine nature, and thereby saints in very truth. They are obliged consequently to retain the holiness they have received as God's gift in the life they lead, to bring it to perfection. They are advised by the apostle, to live 'as is becoming to saints' (Eph. 5:3); 'as God's chosen people, holy and well-beloved', to*

[1] Cf. Origen, *Comm. Rom.* 7, 7: PG 14, 1122 B. Ps.-Macarius, *De Oratione*, 11: PG 34, 861 AB. St Thomas, *Summa Theol.* II-II. a. 184, a. 3.

wear the livery of 'tender compassion, kindness, humility, gentleness and patience' (Col. 3:12); to possess the harvest of the spirit in sanctification (cf. Gal. 5:22; Rom. 6:22). Since we are betrayed, all of us, into many faults (cf. Jas. 3:2), we have a continual need of the mercy of God; our daily prayer must be: 'And forgive us our trespasses' (Matt. 6:12).[1]

It is obvious then to all that all of Christ's faithful, no matter what their rank or station, have a vocation to the fullness of the Christian life and the perfection of charity[2] *and that this sanctity results in the promotion of a more humane way of life even in society on earth. The faithful must exert all the strength they have received, in the measure in which Christ makes his gift, so that they may acquire this perfection. They must follow Christ's footsteps, be moulded to his likeness, be attentive to the will of the Father in all things, be whole-heartedly devoted to the glory of God and the service of their neighbour. This is the way in which an abundant harvest will grow from the holiness of God's people, as is shown brilliantly in the history of the Church by the lives of so many saints* (article 40).

These detailed comments are closely bound up with articles 6-8 of the decree, which deal with the renewal of the Church, the conversion of the heart and unanimous prayer; and with article 4, which also speaks of renewal and offers a reminder that everything produced by the Holy Spirit in the hearts of separated Christians can also serve for our own

[1] Cf. St Augustine, *Retract.* II, 18: PL 32, 637 f.—Pius XII, Encycl. *Mystici Corporis*, 29 June 1943: AAS 35 (1943) p. 225.

[2] Cf. Pius XI, Encycl. *Rerum omnium*, 26 Jan. 1923: AAS 15 (1923) p. 50 and pp. 59-60. Encycl. *Casti Connubii*, 31 Dec. 1930: AAS 22 (1930) p. 548. Pius XII, Apostolic Constitution *Provida Mater*, 2 Feb. 1947: AAS 39 (1947) p. 117. Allocution *Annus sacer*, 8 Dec. 1950: AAS 43 (1951) pp. 27-8. Allocution *Nel darvi*, I July 1956: AAS 48 (1956) p. 574 f.

edification. Both the constitution and the decree refer to several hopeful signs such as the lay apostolate and the spirituality of marriage, which are very promising omens for the renewal of the Church and the future progress of ecumenism. And while article 42 of the constitution exalts martyrdom as the supreme witness of love, article 4 of the decree says that separated Christians have borne witness to Christ even to the shedding of their blood. Article 14 of the decree says of the separated Eastern Churches that they have suffered much, and even today are still suffering, in order to preserve the faith proclaimed by the very earliest Councils.

While article 41 of the constitution gives a description of exemplary Christian life in various spheres of activity, article 15 of the decree deals with the traditions of spirituality in the separated Eastern Churches, and article 23 with the Christian life of separated Christians in the West, especially among the Protestant denominations.

6. Chapter Six: Religious

Article 43 of the constitution says:

The evangelical counsels, consisting of vows to God of chastity, poverty and obedience, are a divine gift which the Church has received from her Lord and always preserved by his grace. They have their foundation in the Lord's words and example; they have the recommendation of the apostles, fathers, doctors of the Church and pastors. Under the guidance of the Holy Spirit, the Church has looked to their elucidation, the control of their practice and the establishment of stable rules for living by them. The result has been as if a tree had grown from the seed God gave and sent out its branches in a striking manner in many quarters of God's field. There has come about the growth of different rules of life, solitary or in community.

Article 44 speaks of the prophetic duty of the religious state within the Church:

The profession of the evangelical counsels is seen to be like a sign which has the power of effectively attracting all the Church's members to a lively performance of the duties of the Christian vocation. The People of God have here no abiding city; they are seeking rather the city that is to come. The religious state, while giving its followers greater independence of earthly cares, gives all believers a clearer demonstration of the truth that the good things of heaven are already present in this age. It also bears a greater witness to the gaining of the new, eternal life which comes from

Christ's redemption; it gives notice of the resurrection to come and the glory of the kingdom in heaven. It is a closer imitation, a perpetual presentation in the Church of the way of life, which the Son of God took up on his entry into the world to do the Father's will, and which he proposed to the disciples, his followers. To sum up, it has a particular way of bringing to light the kingdom of God in its elevated position above all earthly goods and the supremacy of its requirements; it shows all men the massive dominance of Christ's rule, and the unlimited nature of the Holy Spirit's power at work in the Church in a remarkable way.

Article 15 of the decree deals with Eastern monasticism and its spirituality, which 'has been the source and wellspring of the formation of the religious life among the Latins, and has repeatedly been a force of re-invigoration'.

Here again the connexion between the two conciliar documents can be clearly seen.

7. Chapter Seven: The Pilgrim Church's Characteristic Attitude of Expectancy and Her Connexion with the Church in Heaven

CARDINAL SANTOS, Archbishop of Manila, in his *relatio* on this chapter, said that the Fathers of the Council had praised the draft of this chapter during the discussion 'because of its solid, balanced teaching on this theme, which up to now has never been treated synthetically in any doctrinal document. It was praised also because of its careful emphasis on pastoral aspects and the ecumenical attitude which is being proclaimed to our separated brethren in both East and West.' The eschatological character of the Church is the strongest motive for her perpetual self-renewal, which at present is being realized through her ecumenical activity.

The final version takes special account of two of the proposals put forward by the Fathers: the collective, ecclesiastical and cosmic aspect of our eschatological existence is even more strongly emphasized. The *relatio* to article 48 says: 'The eschatological character of the Church is therefore thoroughly treated, not only with regard to its glorified state but also with regard to the pilgrim Church during the time until Christ's coming. This earthly condition manifests not only its real, though still incomplete, renewal, but also the transitory character of the different ecclesiastical institutions and even of the necessary duties which must be fulfilled by the faithful in their work in this world.' All ecclesiastical institutions are provisional and transitory insofar as they will last only until Christ's coming.

A second wish expressed by many of the Fathers was for a clearer delineation of the operation of the Holy Spirit in the pilgrim Church, guiding her on her way to her eschatological fulfilment.

The pilgrim Church exists in an astonishing position between 'already' and 'not yet', as Oscar Cullmann has very expressively put it. The power of Christ's resurrection is already at work in her, and the making new of all things in her has already begun, but in her sacraments and institutions she bears the forms of this transitory life and longs for her fulfilment at Christ's coming.

The promised restoration to which we look forward, has already had its beginning in Christ. It receives impetus on the sending of the Holy Spirit and is continued by his efforts in the Church, where we also receive instruction, by faith, in the significance of our earthly life. We meanwhile, in expectation of a good future, are bringing to completion the work entrusted to us by the Father, and are working to earn our salvation (cf. Phil. 2:12).

The fulfilment of history has already reached us (cf. 1 Cor. 10:11) and the world is irrevocably set on the renewal which is anticipated in a real way in this life. Already the Church is marked on earth by a genuine, if imperfect, holiness. The Church is on pilgrimage until the coming of the new heavens and the new earth, the dwelling-place of holiness (cf. 2 Pet. 3:13). In her sacraments and organization, which belong to this life, she is wearing this age's fashion, a transient mode, and she spends her time surrounded by creatures who groan in travail, as they wait for the sons of God to be made known (cf. Rom. 8:19-22) (article 48).

In the time between the first Pentecost and the coming of its Lord the pilgrim Church is firmly united in a community of spiritual goods with the Church in heaven. The saints are not merely intercessors or examples to copy, they also lead us to Christ, and the purpose of all honour paid to them is ultimately Christ-centred. Veneration of the saints finds its most forceful expression in the celebration of the liturgy, and especially in the eucharist.

We reach the highest degree of union with the worship of the Church in heaven at our celebration of the Mass, as in the fellowship of communion we honour and remember first of all the glorious Mary ever virgin, then we recall the blessed Joseph and the blessed apostles, martyrs and all saints[1] (article 50).

This view, which embraces at once both heaven and earth has been taken up again by article 5 of the decree 'On Ecumenism' in a way especially dear to Eastern Christians.

The *relatio* was right to stress the ecumenical significance of the whole of Chapter seven of the constitution, for it corresponds to the eschatological view of the Church which forms one of the principal themes of the decree.

[1] Canon of the Roman Mass.

8. Chapter Eight: The Blessed Virgin Mary, Mother of God, in the Mystery of Christ and the Church

ON 29 OCTOBER, 1963 the General Congregation, by the narrow margin of 1114 votes to 1074, decided in favour of incorporating the already prepared schema *De Beata Maria Virgine Matre Dei et Matre Hominum* as a separate chapter in the schema 'On the Church'. The schema dealt principally with the privileged graces bestowed on the Mother of God; if it was to be included in the schema 'On the Church' it would need to be adapted to the context of the history of salvation. It is impossible to consider the relation of Mary to the Church without explaining her part in the order of salvation instituted by Jesus Christ. The relation Mary bears to us and to the Church is based on the relation she bore to her Son Jesus Christ. It is in this connexion that her importance as mother of the redeemer and as mother of the redeemed is given such prominence. This position as mother is bound up with her position as a type and image of the Church:

In view of her Son's merits, she was redeemed in a more exalted manner, she was tied to him tightly, with a permanent bond, she is endowed with the office and dignity of being the Mother of God the Son; she is therefore the daughter to whom the Father has shown surpassing love, she is the shrine of the Holy Spirit. This gift of outstanding grace makes her outstrip by far all other creatures in excellence, whether they are in heaven or on earth. At the same time she is to be found linked, in Adam's stock, to all men in need of salvation; or rather, she is 'clearly mother of the members (of Christ) . . . for she has with love co-operated in the birth of the faithful in the Church, and they are the members of that head'.[1] *She is hailed for this reason as eminent above all, and as a wholly unique member of the Church, as the type of the Church in her faith and charity and its most honoured model. The Catholic Church, under the instruction of the Holy Spirit, honours her as its most loving mother with all the affection of a son's love for his mother (article 53).*

In the clause, 'The Catholic Church, under the instruction of the Holy Spirit, honours her as its most loving mother with all the affection of a son's love for his mother', the honorary title *Mater Ecclesiae*, which is commented on in seven other places, is already being implied. Thus article 60 speaks of Mary's 'function as mother', and article 61, after describing her importance in the work of salvation, says: 'This is the reason why she has been our mother in the order of grace'; and article 62 continues: 'Mary's motherhood in the economy of grace has no pause in its duration . . . Raised into heaven, she has not laid aside this saving office but she persists, with many pleas, in winning us the gifts of divine salvation.'

In the *relatio generalis* to chapter eight it says: 'In the title "Mother of the Church" the word "Church" is evidently to be understood as the community of pastors and faithful together, but not as Christ's own act of institution.' The distinction between the Church as the people of God, the

[1] St Augustine, *De S. Virginitate*, 6: PL 40, 399.

totality of the faithful together with their pastors, and the Church as an institution was expressed several times by Paul VI during the concluding days of the Council session while receiving individual groups of bishops. At the general audience on 18 November, 1964 he said: 'Mary has been accorded a unique position. She, too, is a member of the Church, she, too, has been redeemed by Christ. She is our sister. But because of her election as Mother of the redeemer, and because she represents mankind in a perfect and unique way, there is good reason to call her, morally and in the archetypal sense, the Mother of all men, and especially of ourselves, the redeemed and the faithful: the Mother of the faithful, the Mother of the Church.' When Paul VI proclaimed the title *Mater Ecclesiae* on 21 November, 1964 in the aula of the Council, he said: 'Therefore to the glory of the Blessed Virgin and for our own consolation, we declare the most Holy Mary to be the Mother of the Church, that is, of the whole Christian people, the faithful and their pastors alike, who call her their most loving Mother.'

On Sunday, 22 November, 1964, Paul VI took the opportunity to explain the title Mother of the Church to the faithful assembled in St Peter's square, just before the Angelus was said. He urged the veneration of the most Blessed Virgin 'as the loving mother of all the faithful, of all of us, not only as isolated individuals but also as a pilgrim community moving towards its eternal goal'.

The ecumenical significance of Marian devotion is stated in the final article:

It gives the sacred Synod great joy and consolation to observe that among the separated brethren also there are those who give due honour to the Lord and Saviour's Mother, especially among

*Eastern Christians who assemble for the veneration of the ever
virgin Mother of God with impulsive fervour and heart's devotion*[1]
(article 69).

Article 15 of the decree 'On Ecumenism' speaks very
highly of Marian devotion among the separated Eastern
Christians and calls special attention to the connexion
between the title *Dei Genetrix*, defined by the Council of
Ephesus, and the nature of the incarnate Word, at once truly
divine and truly human, just as the constitution *De Ecclesia*
itself does.

It is significant that the decree connects the Mariology of
the Eastern Churches very closely with liturgical worship
and especially with the celebration of the eucharist. In order
to establish the connexion between the chapters on Mary
with the teaching of the Church, several of the Fathers
pointed to the canon of the Roman Mass: 'United in one
fellowship, we reverently call to mind, first, the glorious
ever-virgin Mary, mother of our God and Lord Jesus Christ
... and all your saints.' The Council met this suggestion in
the Prooemium to chapter eight. Joseph Ratzinger observes on
this: 'Since one of the most important achievements of the
constitution has been to restore the idea of the Church as
centred round the liturgy—or in different words, to interpret
the liturgy as the actualization of what the Church is and
ought to be—then this is undoubtedly a perfectly legitimate
point of departure. It serves at the same time to reveal the
underlying foundation of Mariology itself. Mariology is an
intrinsic part of the genuine and, indeed, unique worship of
the Church.'

[1] Cf. Pius XI, Encycl. *Ecclesiam Dei*, 12 Nov. 1923: AAS 15 (1923) p. 581.
Pius XII, Encycl. *Fulgens corona*, 8 Sept. 1953: AAS 45 (1953) pp. 590-1.

It is, in fact, this aspect which gives the Marian devotion of the East its distinctive character and authenticity. The constitution *De Ecclesia* has cited Eastern Fathers and theologians in many places, but it could well have shown more clearly how far it was in agreement with the tradition of the Eastern Churches.

For this reason Antoine Wenger, in his *Chronique de la troisième session* (Paris, 1965, pp. 122-39), has adduced numerous witnesses from Eastern theology to the doctrine of Mary as the Mother of all the faithful, the Mother of the apostles and the pastors of the Church, and the Mother of the *Pleroma Christi*. In the most ancient Greek *Dormitio Mariae*, dating from the end of the fifth century, and translated into Latin in the eighth century, Mary is called 'our sister, who has become the mother of all the world'. Bishop Theoteknos, who was Bishop of Livias in Palestine around A.D. 600, speaks, in much the same terms as the constitution, of Mary's motherly intercession and meditation with her Son. The exposition of Mary's universal motherhood and her mediatorial intercession is reached in the theology of the Metropolitan Theophanes of Nicaea, who died in 1480 or 1481.

Wenger concluded his astonishing list of sources with the words: 'We did not cite these audacious texts with any intention of discovering the universal and definite teaching of the Church. We wished only to show how far the Byzantine tradition has explored the riches of the mystery of Mary and her relation to Christ. Since all theology today must be ecumenical it is only right that Mariology should examine the privileged witnesses of the East in order to learn from them how much more the living written tradition of the Church tells us than literal interpretation of scripture isolated from this tradition.'

Article 20 of the decree 'On Ecumenism' points out that Mariology brings to light decisive doctrinal differences with the Protestant denominations. There is a connexion between the differences about 'Mary's function in the work of salvation' and the disagreements 'on the subject of Christ, the incarnate Word of God, and on the work of redemption, as well as the mystery and the ministry of the Church', as the decree indicates in the same article, without, however, going any more closely into the nature of this connexion.

Conclusion

THE ECCLESIOLOGY of the constitution, which forms the basis of the decree 'On Ecumenism', proceeds from the central concept of communion. All the individual structural elements of the Church are seen under the aspect of communion, in accordance with the theology of the Fathers in both East and West.

Observers from the Protestant denominations spoke of their predilection for a conception of the Church proceeding from the proposition of St Irenaeus: 'Where the Church is, there also is the Spirit of God, and where the Spirit of God is, there is the Church and all grace (*Adv. haer.*, III, 24). Proceeding from the words *ubi Spiritus ibi Ecclesia*, it would be possible to represent all the constitutive elements of the Church in their relation to the Holy Spirit who is the principle of their unity. The constitution meets with these wishes to the extent that the pneumatological aspect is emphasized in many places.

To describe the ecclesiological status of communities separated from the *Sedes Apostolica Romana*, article 8 of the constitution says: 'Christ's only Church has its existence in the Catholic Church ... although outside her framework there are found many elements of holiness and truth...' The structural elements which are present outside the Catholic Church such as it is ordered and constituted in this world are more closely described in article 15, and their ecclesial significance more explicitly indicated. Two points should be noted:

1. The expression *elementa* should not give rise to any idea that we consider the separated churches and ecclesiastical communities as a simple addition of various different elements. The Fathers of the Council were warned of this danger in the 77th General Congregation on 28 November, 1963 by Bishop Émile Blanchet, Rector of the Institut Catholique de Paris. He stressed that it must always be borne in mind that beliefs of separated Christians could not be reduced to a series of propositions which might be sufficiently refuted by a few good arguments. There was something more fundamental behind these propositions: a special view of Christian truth from which everything else proceeded. For this reason article 19 of the decree says that the difference between the Protestant denominations and the Catholic Church is ultimately to be found in a different interpretation of the truths of revelation.

2. When reference is made to 'elements' in the separated Churches and ecclesiastical communities, these should not be thought of merely as 'static' entities—they must also be understood in a 'dynamic' way. Article 15 of the constitution says that the Holy Spirit is working through them and urging them to the fullness of unity desired by Christ. The ecclesial elements are already effecting a certain limited degree of unity with the Catholic Church; they are vital elements proceeding from Christ and leading back to him. In its commentary on this, the decree makes frequent use of the expressions 'life' and 'movement' in order to stress

the dynamic aspect. During the discussion of the schema 'On Ecumenism' during the second session Archbishop George Flahiff of Winnipeg, Canada, declared: 'The dynamic view, which illuminates the Word of the Holy Spirit, seems to me to be more important for an understanding of the ecumenical movement than a mere enumeration of ecclesial values which other churches have preserved. In our ecumenical work the Spirit of God himself produces the various fruits as he will and leads all Christians to a greater fidelity to the divine will.'

The constitution *De Ecclesia* and the decree *De Oecumenismo* clearly have an inner unity. The constitution is a document of dogmatic teaching and as such carries greater weight; its content is more extensive and manifests the catholicity and apostolicity of the Church with the future implications in view. The decree 'On Ecumenism' is a pastoral document which, by giving the teaching of the constitution an ecumenical application, serves to make these teachings more readily understandable.

Article 4 of the constitution sums up the trinitarian view of the Church in the words of Cyprian of Carthage: 'In this way the universal Church is clearly "a people made one with the unity of Father and the Son and the Holy Spirit".' Of this unity, article 2 of the decree says: 'The mystery has its supreme model and its starting point in the unity of Persons in the Trinity, the unity of the one God, Father and Son in the Holy Spirit.'

Postscript

THE SOLEMN promulgation of the decree 'On Ecumenism' at the final meeting of the third session of the Council on 21 November, 1964 was a creative act ushering in a new era in the ecumenical activity of the Church. If one remembers the initial drafts leading to the first schema of 1963 and compares them with the final decree the progress is evident. To what is this due?

The pope's address on 29 September, 1963 for the opening of the second session of the Council and 17 October, 1963 to the observer delegates, as well as his speeches and even more his actions during his visit to the Holy Land made it clear that the first version of the schema would have to be surpassed.

The result of the discussion of the first schema in the Council hall pointed in the same direction. The oral and written votes of the Fathers were far more constructive than negative. Their openness to ecumenical questions surpassed all expectations. The Fathers put forward with great frankness the tasks of ecumenism in the renewal of the Church.

Bishop Hermann Volk of Mainz said in the discussion: 'Ecumenism in the Catholic sense must direct its activities not only to the Christians separated from us but also to the Catholic Church itself. For the uniqueness of the Church includes also its catholicity and universality, that is to say all that is truly Christian must have its proper place in the Catholic Church. True, this universality is a gift the Church has received from Christ its Head; but the Church is nevertheless obliged always and in all things to strive for genuine universality, both in its doctrine and in its life. The Church of Christ is capable of acknowledging and accepting whatever is truly Christian and must be prepared to do so. The realization of this catholicity of the Church involves difficult questions. . .'[1]

In his opening speech of the second session of the Council Pope Paul VI described the ecumenical hope and task of the Church in the following terms: 'The Council strives for a full and all-embracing ecumenity, at least in desire, in prayer and in preparation. Today a hope arises, tomorrow this hope may perhaps be realized . . . But we are conscious of the tremendous difficulties that still stand in the way of this unity that is so greatly desired. We put our trust in God. Hence we shall continue to pray and strive to give a better example of true Christian life and brotherly love. If the events should not correspond to our hope and our expectations we shall console ourselves with our Lord's saying: "What is impossible with men is possible with God".'[2]

The decree on ecumenism is animated by the same hope, as is clear from its concluding paragraph. The decree, which was accepted by the Fathers almost unanimously, is indeed new, but it combines continuity and progress, the two principles of the development of the Church's life. Tradition kept alive by the Holy Spirit gives the impulses and sugges-

[1] J. C. Hampe, *Ende der Gegenreformation?* Berlin-Stuttgart and Mainz 1964, 322 f.   [2] Luke 18:27.

tions for the progress of the people of God on its pilgrimage and towards new ecumenical initiatives.

The observer delegates of the non-Catholic churches and communities have made effective contributions to the ecumenical concerns of the Council and especially to the decree 'On Ecumenism'. In an interview given to the Evangelical Press Service in Rome at the conclusion of the third session of the Council on 21 November, 1964 Cardinal Bea stated this explicitly. The Cardinal was asked: 'The non-Catholic asks which spiritual reality lies behind the vote of the Council on the schema "On ecumenism". In view of the fact that this text contains a great many statements which would have been quite unthinkable even ten years ago, especially here in Rome, we should like to ask: Have there been so many changes in these last years or has the Council anticipated future developments with this text?'

Cardinal Bea replied:

'Behind the decree 'On Ecumenism' lies the spiritual reality that has been created by the preparation of the Council and especially by development within the Council itself. Perhaps it is not yet sufficiently realized what great things have been set in motion by the Council, affecting the Churches as well as Catholic and non-Catholic Christians. A twofold encounter has taken place in the Council: the meeting of all Catholic bishops of the world with one another and their meeting with the representatives of so many non-Catholic Churches or world associations of Churches. The effects of this latter encounter can hardly be overestimated and their scope and immense consequences have probably not been sufficiently realized yet. Recently, the well-known French ecumenist Pastor Marc Boegner gave an impressive account of them in a lecture delivered in Rome. I myself can publicly state that the non-Catholic observers have made a decisive contribution to the decree 'On Ecumenism'. True, they did not prepare this decree, they did not participate directly in the debates and the voting of the Council, but their presence at the Council and their participation in it through prayer, study, and various contacts and suggestions have given the Fathers of the Council a deep and many-sided experience of the ecumenical problem. In this way they have become conscious of the unity in Christ that already exists between us, of the many things that separate us, and the tremendous difficulties of ecumenical activity. Perhaps, conversely, the effects of the Council on non-Catholic Christians and their Churches might also be matter for consideration. But now it is probably enough just to have suggested this. The decree 'On Ecumenism' is a concrete written outcome of all these experiences, which in my view are much more important and will bear much more fruit than the decree itself, even though this, too, is of course absolutely necessary.

From what I have said you will see that in the last few years there have indeed been profound changes in the Church, the effects of which will be realized only very gradually. In this respect the experience of the Council by all Christians together may be compared to the mustard seed of the gospel, which grows slowly until at last it is visible in all its size and importance.

On the other hand you are right to suggest that the

decree *also* anticipates developments. Perhaps it is more accurate to say that it is a 'foresight and anticipation'. And why not? If every prudent lawgiver must somehow foresee and provide for further developments, then the same may and must be assumed of the legislating body of the Church. Here foresight is easier because the whole work of the Council is aided by the powerful divine action of the Spirit of Christ, who is planning for the Church and who is the chief worker in the Council. The tremendous changes just mentioned have taken place under the inspiration of this Spirit, and under his guidance the Council has tried to foresee the future development and to give it its direction.[1]

The last words of the decree, which hold so much promise for the future, must be seen in this perspective: the Council does not wish to hinder the inscrutable ways of Providence and the future impulses of the Holy Spirit. During the second session Archbishop Andreas Pangrazio of Gorize gave the reason for this trusting attitude:

In the history of the Church events, whether assisted or resisted by men, take place often in a totally unexpected way, which no theological system can foresee or understand. Which of the great thirteenth-century theologians, for example, could have dreamed of that Western schism which tore the Church apart in the fourteenth century, or the malformations and abuses that marred the appearance of the Church before the Reformation? On the other hand, who could have foretold the marvellous recovery

[1] *Evangelischer Pressedienst*, 21 November, 1964, p. 2 f.

which God was working in his Church after the Council of Trent?

This view of the mysterious quality of Church history seems to me highly important for Catholic ecumenism. For just as God's people in the Old Covenant knew his merciful intention through revelation and could and should always hope that he would turn its history from misfortune to a happy outcome, so the people of the New Testament, too, must hope that by the grace of his mercy God will lead his Church in an as yet unknown manner on ways that none of us can foresee or predict . . .

For this reason God can make possible the desired unity of divided Christendom which today still seems impossible to us, if only all Christians follow the impulses of divine grace.

We must remind ourselves again and again that it is the Holy Spirit, Creator, Lord and Lifegiver, who leads the pilgrim people of God to perfection. It is a special merit of the decree 'On Ecumenism' that it emphasizes so strongly the workings of the Holy Spirit in the Church and in Christendom. The pneumatological motif is sounded in the Introduction and penetrates the whole text right through to the conclusion, ending in the last word on the great hope of Christendom: 'Nor does this hope delude us: the love of God has been poured out in our hearts by the Holy Spirit, whom we have received' (Rom. 5:5).

Appendix

THE SOURCES used in working out the versions of the schema
'On Ecumenism' up to the final text of the decree are very
important for scholarly research on it. They can be divided
into the following groups:

1. Quotations from scripture, the Fathers of the Church
and earlier Councils which are named in the text itself or
in the notes to the decree and hence are not listed here.

2. Official pronouncements of the popes and the Roman
authorities as well as theological publications which were
used while the schema was being worked out. These are
given in Latin in the German edition; here we give only
either the references themselves or a brief English résumé
of the contents. Many of these sources are concerned with
the Eastern Churches separated from us. On 18 November,
1963 Archbishop Martin said in his *relatio* on the first version
of the schema: 'Everything here said of the Eastern Churches
separated from Rome is said because it is true and right,
whether it concerns their history, their venerable traditions
dating from the time of the apostles and the Fathers of the
Church, their special spirituality and similar matters. But
what is said about these Churches is often confirmed by
quotations from Leo XIII and Pius XII in order to make

it clear that the statements of the decree are made not out of opportunism but in harmony with the doctrine of those popes who enjoy a special reputation in our time.'

3. Of the *vota* of the Council Fathers proposed during the discussion of the schema 'On Ecumenism' we only give a few examples. The others have appeared in *Osservatore Romano* and in the communications of the press office of the Vatican Council.

Herder Correspondence (1963-4) published an informative article on the first version of the schema 'On Ecumenism' and a detailed account of its discussion during the second session of the Council. The results of this discussion with regard to the individual chapters of the schema are treated by E. Stakemeier in his essay on 'Die Konzilsdiskussion über das Schema *De Oecumenismo*. Eine Übersicht über die Ergebnisse', in *Theologie und Glaube* 54 (1964) 161-81. After the conclusion of the second session several works on the discussions of the schema 'On Ecumenism' were published, for example, Raniero La Valle, *Coraggio del Concilio, giorno per giorno la seconda sessione*, Brescia 1964, 343-455; A. Wenger, *Vatican II, Chronique de la deuxième session*, Paris 1964, 172-218; R. Laurentin, *L'enjeu du Concile; Bilan de la deuxième session 29 septembre-4 décembre 1963*, Paris 1964, 145-64; 234-7; W. Seibel, S. J., L. A. Dorn, *Tagebuch des Konzils. Die Arbeit der zweiten Session*, Nuremberg 1964 (contains the Information Service for Council Fathers edited by the Centrum Informationis Catholicum in Rome during the second Session of the Council). The text of the decree shows that not all the proposals and wishes of the *vota* here quoted as sources were accepted by the Council. For example the decree has refrained from including an actual 'theology of the divisions' which had been suggested.

4. Since we have confined ourselves to describing the preparation, discussion and final issue of the decree we cannot deal with the sources used in the more remote preparation of the decree by the Secretariat for Christian Unity before the opening of the Council. But we remember gratefully the frequently difficult preparatory work of theologians and laymen whom one might call the pioneers of ecumenism.

ARTICLE 1

Preface

John XXIII, Litt. Encycl. *Ad Petri Cathedram*, 29 June, 1959, AAS 51 (1959) 511, 516.

John XXIII, Motu Proprio *Superno Dei nutu*, 5 June, 1960, ASS 52 (1960) 436. Institution of the Secretariat for Christian Unity.

John XXIII, Const. Apost. *Humane Salutis*, 25 December, 1961, which announces the Second Vatican Council, AAS 54 (1962) p. 9.

Paul VI, *Allocution to Council Fathers*, 29 September, 1963, AAS 55 (1963) 852.

ARTICLE 2

The Unity and Oneness of the Church

Leo XIII, Epist. Encycl. *Satis cognitum*, 29 June, 1896, ASS 28 (1895-6) 710. Unity of the Church divinely instituted.

ARTICLE 3

The Relation of the Separated Brethren to the Catholic Church

John XXIII, Litt. Encycl. *Ad Petri Cathedram*, 29 June, 1959, AAS (1959) 515. Those separated from us are to be addressed as brothers.

Pius XII, *Alacre Studium*, AAS 37 (1945) 600.

Card. C. Journet, *L'Eglise du Verbe Incarné I, La Hiérarchie Apostolique II*, 1955, p. 652, on valid orders in separated Churches. Quotes on this question L. Billot, *De Ecclesia Christi*, Rome 1921, 339.

On all dissident Christian communities

Leo XIII, *Epist. Longinqua Oceani*, 6 January 1895, ASS 27 (1894-5) 399.

Leo XIII, *Epist. Caritatis studium*, 25 July 1898, ASS 31 (1898-9) 11.

Pius XI, *Litt. Encycl. Lux veritatis*, 25 December 1931, AAS 23 (1939) 510.

J. Gribomont, OSB, 'Du Sacrement de l'Eglise et de ses réalisations imparfaites', in *Irenikon* 22 (1949) 356.

In the tradition of the Church the term Church is often and constantly given to the Eastern separated communities; cf. the following ecclesiastical documents:

1074-6, St. Gregory VII speaks of the 'Constantinopolitan Church' (Migne, PL 148, 385-7) and of the 'Eastern Church', (ibid. 399 f).

1095, Urban II 'the liberation of the Eastern Churches' (thus Villey, *La Croisade*, 81).

1215, Fourth Lateran Council, 'The Church of the Greeks' (Mansi 22, 989); so also Gregory IX (Mansi 23, 58A, C, E and 59, B and C).

1274, Second Council of Lyons; (see Mansi 24, 70A).

1439, Council of Florence, in definition *Laetentur caeli* of 6 July, 1439, 'the Eastern Church', (in *Conciliorum Oecumenicorum Decreta*, Herder 1962, 500).

1848, Pius IX in Litt. ad Orientales, *In Suprema*, 6 January 1848, (Pii IX P.M. Acta vol. 1, 85).

1867, Pius IX, in *Alloc.* in Consistorio circa patriarchatum Ciliciae Armenorum, 12 July, 1867, (AAS 3 (1867) 345).

1868, Pius IX, *Arcano divinae Providentiae*, 'Churches of the Eastern rite', ASS 4 (1868) 129-31.

1894, Leo XIII, Epist. Apost. *Praeclarae gratulationis*, 20 June, 1894, 'Eastern Churches', (ASS 26 (1893-4) 709).

1898, Leo XIII, Litt. Apost. *Cum divini Pastoris*, 25 May, 1898, (Acta 18 (1898) 49).

1907, S.C. Indulgentiarum, 'dissident Churches'.

1912, S. Pius X, Const. Apost. *Tradita ab antiquis*, 14 September, 1912, (AAS 4 (1912) 610).

1920, Benedict XV, Litt. Encycl. *Spiritus Paraclitus*, 15 September, 1920, (AAS (1920) 421).

1924, Pius XI, in *Alloc.* in Consistorio, 18 December, 1924, (AAS 16 (1924) 491).

1928, Pius XI, Litt. Encycl. *Mortalium animos*, 6 January, 1928, 'Christian Churches', though more in sociological sense (AAS 20 (1928) 9).

1944, Pius XII, Litt. Encycl. *Orientalis Ecclesiae decus*, 9 April, 1944, calls several separated Eastern communities Eastern Churches, (AAS 36 (1944) 129 ff).

1945, Pius XII, Litt. Encycl. *Orientales omnes Ecclesias*, 23 December, 1945 (AAS 38 (1946) 33).

1953, Pius XII, Litt. Encycl. *Orientales Ecclesias*, 15 December, 1952, (AAS 45 (1953) 5).

1961, John XXIII, Litt. Encycl. *Aeterna Dei sapientia*, 21 November, 1961, (AAS 53 (1961) 790).

1963, Paul VI, in sermon at monastery of Cryptoferrata, 18 August, 1963, speaks of separated Eastern Churches, (*Osservatore Romano* 19-20 August, 1963).

1963, Paul VI, in *Alloc.* to Council Fathers, 29 September, 1963, (AAS 55 (1963) 859).

1964, Paul VI, in sermon delivered at Bethlehem on 6 January, 1964, (AAS 56 (1964) 176). S.C.E. Officii, *Letter* to Cardinal Archbishop Cushing of Boston, 8 August, 1949, (in *The American Ecclesiastical Review* 127 (Oct. 1952) 308).

ARTICLE 4

Ecumenism

S.C.S. Officii, *Instr. De motione oecumenica*, 20 December, 1949, (AAS 42 (1950) 142 and 147).

John XXIII, *Allocutio* Capitulo Generalis Congregationis Ss. mi Sacramenti, (*Osservatore Romano*, 30 June, 1961).

Cf. Pius XI, In Audience, 9 January, 1927, (*Osservatore Romano* 10-11 Jan. 1927).

ARTICLE 5

The Care for the Restoration of Unity Belongs to the Whole Church

Augustine Cardinal Bea, 'Clarifications', *Council Speeches of Vatican II*, London, 1964, 109-11.

Charles de Provenchères, Archbishop of Aix-en-Provence, 'Erneuerung der ganzen Kirche' publ. in J. C. Hampe, *Ende der Gegenreformation? Das Konzil. Dokumente und Deutung*, 1964, 316-18.

Hermann Volk, Bishop of Mainz, 'Was heisst für die katholische Kirche ökumenisch sein?' in J. C. Hampe, loc. cit. 322-5.

ARTICLE 6

The Renewal of the Church

John XXIII, Litt. Encycl. *Ad Petri Cathedram*, 29 June, 1959, (AAS 51 (1959) 511). Announces Council for the renewal of the Church.

Innocent III, *Sermon VI* delivered at General Council of the Lateran, (PL 217, 674); this Council called for the reform of the universal Church and the liberation of the Holy Land.

Fifth Lateran Council, session 12, 16 March, 1517, (in *Conciliorum Oecumenicorum Decreta*, Herder 1962, 626 f).

Paul VI, *Alloc.* ad Curiam Romanam, 21 September, 1963, (AAS 55 (1963) 797): constant reform of Church necessary insofar as it is a human institution.

John XXIII, *Concilium Oecumenicum Vat. II* sollemniter inchoatur, (AAS 54 (1962) 792).

ARTICLE 7

The Conversion of the Heart

Paul VI, Opening speech of the second session of Vatican II (in Congar, *Report from Rome II*, op. cit., 133-59).

Address to the Observers, 17 October, 1963 (in *Report from Rome II*, op. cit., 160-70).

Cardinal J. Humberto Quintero, Archbishop of Caracas, 'Confiteor', (in *Council Speeches*, op. cit., 98-9).

Charles-Marie Himmer, Bishop of Tournay, (in J. C. Hampe, 334-6).

Cardinal E. Ruffini, Archbishop of Palermo, ibid. 344 f.

ARTICLE 8

Unanimous Prayer

Joseph Tawil, Greek-Melchite Vicar Patriarch in Egypt, (in *Council Speeches*, op. cit., 127-9).

Gerard Huyghe, Bishop of Arras, (ibid. 130-3 ff).

ARTICLE 9

The Mutual Knowledge of the Brethren

Pius XII, Litt. Encycl. *Sempiternus Rex* of 8 September, 1951, (AAS 43 (1951) 642).

S.C.S. Officii, *Instr. De motione oecumenica*, (ASS 42 (1950) 145).

A. Cardinal Bea, 'Clarifications' (in *Council Speeches*, op. cit., 109-11).

Casimiro Morcillo, Archbishop of Saragossa, (ibid. 102-5).

John Carmel Heenan, Cardinal-Archbishop of Westminster, 'Ecumenism in England' (ibid. 106-8).

Paul Gouyon, Coadjutor-Archbishop of Rennes.

E. Blanchet, Rector of the Institut Catholique in Paris, ibid. 154-7.

ARTICLE 10

Ecumenical Instruction

Cardinal Paul Emile Léger, ibid. 147-9.
Eugene D'Souza, Archbishop of Bhopal, ibid. 140-2.

ARTICLE 11

The Way in which the Doctrine of Fatih is Expressed and Presented

S.C.S. Officii, *Instr. De motione oecumenica*, (AAS 42 (1950) 144), warns against watering down Catholic doctrine.

Paul VI, Address to Observers, 17 October, 1963, (in *Report from Rome*, op. cit.).

Benedict Reetz, Archabbot of Beuron, 'Steine des Anstosses', in Hampe, loc. cit. 341-3.

ARTICLE 12

Co-operation with the Separated Brethren

S.C.S. Officii, *Instr. De motione oecumenica*, (AAS 42 (1950) 145).

Cardinal Valerian Gracias, Archbishop of Bombay, (in *Council Speeches*, pp. 151-4).

Cardinal Laurean Rugambwa, Bishop of Bukoba, (in J. C. Hampe) 311.

Jean Baptiste Zoa, Archbishop of Yaoundé, (in *Council Speeches*, pp. 184-5).

Franz Hengsbach, Bishop of Essen, 'On Collaboration with the separated Brethren', (in J. C. Hampe, 337).

ARTICLE 13

The Two Great Divisions of the Church

George Flahiff, Archbishop of Winnipeg, (in *Council Speeches*, 122-3).

Joseph Tawil, Hampe, 327.

ARTICLE 14

The Attitude and History Proper to the Easterns

Cf. G. L. Hertling, S.J., *Communio, Chiesa e Papato nell' antichità cristiana*, Rome, 1961.

Cf. also G. Bardy, *La théologie de l'Eglise de Saint Clément de Rome à Saint Irénée*, Paris 1945.

Leo XIII, Litt. Apost. *Orientalium Dignitas*, 30 November, 1894, (AAS 27 (1894-5) 258), emphasizes common origin and relation between Eastern Churches and Rome.

Leo XIII, ibid. 257, praises doctrine and sanctity of early Eastern Church.

ARTICLE 15

The Liturgical and Spiritual Traditions of the Easterns

Cf. St John Chrysostom, *Homily 46 on John*, PG 59, 260-2.

Cf. Pius XII, *Allocution* of 11 April, 1958, (AAS 50 (1958) 282-6): Eastern monasticism the origin of Western religious life, its influence to be found in almost all the great religious Orders.

ARTICLE 16

The Discipline Proper to the Easterns

Leo XIII, Litt. Apost. *Orientalium Dignitas*, (AAS 27 (1894-6) 258).

Id. Motu proprio *Auspicia rerum*, 19 March, 1896, (AAS 28 (1895-6) 589).

ARTICLE 17

The Special Characteristics of the Easterns in Treating Divine Doctrine

Pius XII, Litt. Encycl. *Orientalis Ecclesiae decus*, 9 April, 1944, (AAS (1944) 137 f.).

Legitimate freedom of Eastern Churches to be preserved as long as they do not deviate from integral Christian doctrine.

ARTICLE 18

Conclusion

Elias Zoghby, Greek-Melchite Patriarchal Vicar in Egypt, (in *Council Speeches*, 32-5).

Gerard Huyghe, Bishop of Arras, ibid. 130-3.

ARTICLE 19

The Special Situation of the Separated Churches and Ecclesial Communities in the West

Kristen E. Skydsgaard, Address to Pope Paul VI on behalf of the guests and observers, 17 October, 1963, (in *Report from Rome*, op. cit. 162-5).

Paul VI, Address to the observer delegates and guests, 17 October, 1963, (ibid. 166-70).

Joseph-Marie Martin, Archbishop of Rouen, *relatio* on the schema 'On Ecumenism', (in Hampe 288-90).

Paul Gouyon, Coadjutor-Archbishop of Rennes, (in *Council Speeches*, op. cit. 115-17).

Archimandrite Rodopoulos, Address at the reception of the observers by Pope Paul VI, 29 September, 1964.

Paul VI, Address to the observers, 29 September, 1964, both in *Herder Correspodence* 1964-5.

ARTICLE 20

On Confessing Christ

Cf. *The New Delhi Report*, SCM Press 1962, especially the basic formula of the World Council of Churches and the report of the section on unity, 116 ff.

ARTICLE 21

On the Study of Holy Scripture

Sergio Medez Arceo, Bishop of Cuernavaca in Mexico (in *Council Speeches*, 118-21).

J.-M. Martin, *relatio* on the schema 'On Ecumenism' (in Hampe, 290).

ARTICLE 22

On the Sacramental Life

Dogmatic Constitution *De Ecclesia*, c. 2, *On the People of God*, art. 15.

ARTICLE 23

On Life with Christ

Dogmatic Constitution *De Ecclesia*, ibid., art. 15,

ARTICLE 24

Conclusion

Paul VI, Opening speech of the second session of Vatican II, op. cit. 11-13.

Joseph-Marie Martin, *relatio* on the schema 'On Ecumenism', in Hampe, 288-90.

SOURCES FOR ECUMENICAL WORK DURING THE PREPARATION OF THE SECOND VATICAN COUNCIL

Augustin Cardinal Bea, *The Unity of Christians*, London, 1963. The German edition of this book, Freiburg, 1963, gives a bibliographical appendix which lists further contributions to the problem of unity and the publications of the Secretariat for Christian Unity.

Index

Abyssinians, 127

Aegidius of Viterbo, 80

Africa, the Church in, 75

Alexandria, Church at, 131

Anabaptists, 117, 152, 162

Anglican Communion, the, 40, 42, 125, 128–9

Antioch, Church at, 131

Apostles, the, 85–6; Christ's role for, 73; the apostolic succession, 138–9; apostolic tradition, as common source in whole Church, 147–8

Aquinas, St Thomas. *See under* Thomas

Ariccia: plenary session of Secretariat for Unity at, 6, 22–3

Athenagoras, Patriarch of Constantinople: meeting with Paul VI, 6, 69

Augustine, St, 71, 74, 79n, 83, 90, 160, 179, 196n, 209; *De Civitate Dei*, 18; on celebration of the eucharist, 136; on relation of the hierarchy to Unity, 199

Baptism, 43–4, 152, 182, 190, 200; and communion with the Catholic Church, 81; and incorporation in Christ, 82; as sacramental bond of unity, 163–4; doubts on validity of, in some places, 164

Basil, St, 141

Bea, Augustin, Cardinal: as President of Secretariat for Unity, 5, 9, 120; presides over Ariccia session of, 22–3; on relation of the Church to the Jews, 20; *relatio* on first version of *De Oecumenismo*, 21; Munich speech on alterations to second version, 60; on reading the Scriptures under guidance of Holy Spirit, 161–2; lecture on furthering Christian Unity through University research and teaching, 162–3; on contributions made at Vatican Council by non-Catholic observers, 219–20; on changes in the Church, 220–1; *The Unity of Christians*, 236

Benedict, St, 141

Bethlehem, Paul VI's address at, 31

Bible, the, as inspired work of God, 102. *See also* Scripture, Holy

Bishops: recommended to promote ecumenical activity, 97; discussion of in *De Ecclesia*, 194 ff

Blanchet, Emile, Titular Archbishop, on the Reformed Church, 155–6, 215

Bloodshed, in witness to Christ, 99, 202

Boegner, Marc, 220

Brethren, separated. *See* Christians, separated

Bukatko, Coadjutor-Archbishop Gabriel, 36

Caerularius, Michael, Patriarch, 47

Calvin, John, 166, 172

Campeggio, Cardinal, 117

Carli, Bishop, of Segni, 184

Carthage, Synod XVI, 123

Cassian, John, 141

Catholic belief, method and manner of presenting, 112 ff

Catholics: and pastoral purpose of *De Oecumenismo*, 67; and furtherance of ecumenism, 88–9, 172–4; attitude to separated brethren, 94, 97, 106; renewal of life within own Church, 94–5; faults and imperfections of individuals in the Church, 105, 123–4

Chalcedon, Council of, 125, 126–7

Chaldaic Christians, 126

Christ: as corner-stone of the Church, 28; as bond uniting all common elements of churches, 42; revelation accomplished in, 101; the Servant, 118, 120, 199; as Centre, on which depend all Churches, 122; as source of fellowship, 156; faith in, by Protestants, 169–71

Christendom, scandal of divisions in, 25, 30, 64, 78

Christians, non-Catholic: connexion with Church as explained in *De Ecclesia*, 190–2

Christology: different concepts of, 117, 118, 156–7

Chrysostom, St John. *See* John

237